Marin County
305.42 Feminism
Feminism
31111032479022

SERIES

Fe	DATE DUE	

Other Books of Related Interest:

Opposing Viewpoints Series

Male and Female Roles

At Issue Series

Women in Islam

Current Controversies Series

Violence Against Women

"Congress shall make no law . . . abridging the freedom of speech, or of the press."

First Amendment to the US Constitution

The basic foundation of our democracy is the First Amendment guarantee of freedom of expression. The Opposing Viewpoints series is dedicated to the concept of this basic freedom and the idea that it is more important to practice it than to enshrine it.

Feminism

Nancy Dziedzic, Book Editor

GREENHAVEN PRESS
A part of Gale, Cengage Learning

Detroit • New York • San Francisco • New Haven, Conn • Waterville, Maine • London

Elizabeth Des Chenes, *Managing Editor*

© 2012 Greenhaven Press, a part of Gale, Cengage Learning.

Gale and Greenhaven Press are registered trademarks used herein under license.

For more information, contact:
Greenhaven Press
27500 Drake Rd.
Farmington Hills, MI 48331-3535
Or you can visit our Internet site at gale.cengage.com

For product information and technology assistance, contact us at

Gale Customer Support, 1-800-877-4253
For permission to use material from this text or product, submit all requests online at www.cengage.com/permissions

Further permissions questions can be emailed to permissionrequest@cengage.com

Articles in Greenhaven Press anthologies are often edited for length to meet page requirements. In addition, original titles of these works are changed to clearly present the main thesis and to explicitly indicate the author's opinion. Every effort is made to ensure that Greenhaven Press accurately reflects the original intent of the authors. Every effort has been made to trace the owners of copyrighted material.

Cover Image copyright © Thinkstock/Getty Images.

LIBRARY OF CONGRESS CATALOGING-IN-PUBLICATION DATA

Feminism / Nancy Dziedzic, book editor.
    p. cm. -- (Opposing viewpoints)
    Includes bibliographical references and index.
    ISBN 978-0-7377-5440-7 (hbk.) -- ISBN 978-0-7377-5441-4 (pbk.)
    1. Feminism. 2. Women's Rights. I. Dziedzic, Nancy G.
    HQ1155.F442 2012
    305.42--dc23

                                                              2011047669

Printed in the United States of America
1 2 3 4 5 6 7 16 15 14 13 12

Contents

Chapter 3: What Role Does Religion Play in Feminism?

Chapter 4: How Are Sexuality and Reproductive Rights Affected by Feminism?

Why Consider Opposing Viewpoints?

> *"The only way in which a human being can make some approach to knowing the whole of a subject is by hearing what can be said about it by persons of every variety of opinion and studying all modes in which it can be looked at by every character of mind. No wise man ever acquired his wisdom in any mode but this."*
>
> *John Stuart Mill*

In our media-intensive culture it is not difficult to find differing opinions. Thousands of newspapers and magazines and dozens of radio and television talk shows resound with differing points of view. The difficulty lies in deciding which opinion to agree with and which "experts" seem the most credible. The more inundated we become with differing opinions and claims, the more essential it is to hone critical reading and thinking skills to evaluate these ideas. Opposing Viewpoints books address this problem directly by presenting stimulating debates that can be used to enhance and teach these skills. The varied opinions contained in each book examine many different aspects of a single issue. While examining these conveniently edited opposing views, readers can develop critical thinking skills such as the ability to compare and contrast authors' credibility, facts, argumentation styles, use of persuasive techniques, and other stylistic tools. In short, the Opposing Viewpoints Series is an ideal way to attain the higher-level thinking and reading skills so essential in a culture of diverse and contradictory opinions.

In addition to providing a tool for critical thinking, Opposing Viewpoints books challenge readers to question their own strongly held opinions and assumptions. Most people form their opinions on the basis of upbringing, peer pressure, and personal, cultural, or professional bias. By reading carefully balanced opposing views, readers must directly confront new ideas as well as the opinions of those with whom they disagree. This is not to argue simplistically that everyone who reads opposing views will—or should—change his or her opinion. Instead, the series enhances readers' understanding of their own views by encouraging confrontation with opposing ideas. Careful examination of others' views can lead to the readers' understanding of the logical inconsistencies in their own opinions, perspective on why they hold an opinion, and the consideration of the possibility that their opinion requires further evaluation.

Evaluating Other Opinions

To ensure that this type of examination occurs, Opposing Viewpoints books present all types of opinions. Prominent spokespeople on different sides of each issue as well as well-known professionals from many disciplines challenge the reader. An additional goal of the series is to provide a forum for other, less known, or even unpopular viewpoints. The opinion of an ordinary person who has had to make the decision to cut off life support from a terminally ill relative, for example, may be just as valuable and provide just as much insight as a medical ethicist's professional opinion. The editors have two additional purposes in including these less known views. One, the editors encourage readers to respect others' opinions—even when not enhanced by professional credibility. It is only by reading or listening to and objectively evaluating others' ideas that one can determine whether they are worthy of consideration. Two, the inclusion of such viewpoints encourages the important critical thinking skill of objectively evaluating an author's credentials and bias. This evaluation will illuminate an author's reasons for taking a particular stance on an issue and will aid in readers' evaluation of the author's ideas.

It is our hope that these books will give readers a deeper understanding of the issues debated and an appreciation of the complexity of even seemingly simple issues when good and honest people disagree. This awareness is particularly important in a democratic society such as ours in which people enter into public debate to determine the common good. Those with whom one disagrees should not be regarded as enemies but rather as people whose views deserve careful examination and may shed light on one's own.

Thomas Jefferson once said that "difference of opinion leads to inquiry, and inquiry to truth." Jefferson, a broadly educated man, argued that "if a nation expects to be ignorant and free . . . it expects what never was and never will be." As individuals and as a nation, it is imperative that we consider the opinions of others and examine them with skill and discernment. The Opposing Viewpoints series is intended to help readers achieve this goal.

David L. Bender and Bruno Leone,
Founders

Introduction

"Like Broadway, the novel, and God, feminism has been declared dead many times."

—Katha Pollitt,
Reasonable Creatures:
Essays on Women and Feminism

The so-called second wave of feminism began in the early 1960s, coinciding with the publication of Betty Friedan's now classic *The Feminine Mystique*, and lasted until the 1980s. During this time, feminists fought—sometimes on the streets and sometimes in court—for equal pay for equal work, reproductive rights, and an end to discrimination in the workplace and in schools. Among the legal victories achieved during this time was the enactment in 1972 of the law called Title IX. Originally part of the Civil Rights Act of 1964, the later version of Title IX that was passed into law ensured that girls and women would not be barred from participating in educational or extracurricular activities at institutions that received federal funding. The main and most controversial aspect of Title IX was that female students could not be prevented from playing intramural school sports or from forming intramural teams and leagues.

Prior to the passage of Title IX, women's participation in competitive team sports was uncommon. While Smith College in Massachusetts introduced a women's basketball team in 1892 and the All-American Girls Professional Baseball League was instituted in 1943 to replace Major League Baseball's absence during World War II, in general young women and girls had little opportunity to compete on team sports. One notable exception could be found in the amateur sport of roller derby, which had been introduced as a type of sports entertainment and endurance contest during a roller skating craze in the 1920s. Originally performed on a raised, or banked, track, this early form of roller derby included both men and women. In the 1940s roller derby became dominated by women because so many American men were off fighting in World War II. In fact, according to Kara Baumeister in "The History of Women's Roller Derby," the sport reached such popularity that it was first broadcast on television in 1948, before most Americans even had televisions at home.

By the 1970s, however, an element of overt sexuality had crept in, and the entertainment value overtook the athleticism of roller derby. Team uniforms gave way to skimpy costumes, and the women were encouraged to play to a classic good girl/bad girl dichotomy. In 1972—the same year Title IX was signed into law—Hollywood sex symbol Raquel Welch starred in a roller derby–themed film, *Kansas City Bomber*, wearing a famously low-cut satin jacket as part of her uniform. But even with Hollywood backing and a theatrical atmosphere (fights between star performers often were staged for effect), roller derby died out as both a sport and an entertainment and virtually disappeared, except as an example of 1970s kitsch, for the next two decades.

Then in Austin, Texas, in 2001, a group of women formed the Texas Rollergirls. Skating on a flat, rather than raised, track and running the organization themselves as a nonprofit business, the women emphasized the athleticism of early roller derby, and women's leagues sprang up across the country and around the world. According to the Women's Flat Track Derby Association (WFTDA), there were about five hundred flat track roller derby leagues worldwide by 2011, with dozens of additional leagues that compete on the old-style banked tracks. In 2009 Drew Barrymore directed and starred in *Whip It*, another roller derby movie about a small-town Texas teenager, played by Ellen Page, who joins a roller derby team and gets an empowering glimpse of life beyond her stifling world of beauty pageants and maternal expectations.

Modern women's roller derby has reflected the arc, and the controversy, of modern feminism. In the later 1980s and early 1990s a new "wave" of feminism began to emerge—the third wave. While second wave feminists had focused their efforts on achieving collective advancements for women in education, industry, and society through large-scale organized activism, third wave feminists' goals were more individualized; this group of women, most of whom were born in the 1960s and 1970s, explored their personal identity and sexual satisfaction and encouraged the ethnic and sexual diversity that the second wave was often accused of ignoring. While some third wave feminists claimed the characters on the television show *Sex and the City* as role models, others turned to more iconoclastic cultural figures, such as 1950s pinup icon Bettie Page and 1990s feminist punk bands like Bikini Kill and Sleater-Kinney who, with many other female musicians, formed the riot grrrl movement that launched an entire music-centered feminist subculture.

Enter the renaissance of roller derby, which offered the latter type of third wave feminists the opportunity to showcase both their physical athleticism and their riot grrrl–influenced aesthetic. Twenty-first-century roller derby features rockabilly- and punk-inspired fashion, which tends to be self-consciously sexualized to affirm the wearer's ownership of her own sexuality, but the skaters are also athletes who encourage their spectators to take the "bouts" seriously as sport. Despite the sexy costumes, provocative pseudonyms, and overall theatrical nature of roller derby, both skaters and fans insist that competitions are more than mere spectacle. Detractors argue that participants actively demean themselves by wearing revealing costumes and engaging in the kind of girl-on-girl quasi-violence that was used to objectify women skaters back in the 1970s, but fans and skaters insist that modern roller derby is empowering because it defies conventional expectations. Los Angeles blogger Hank Leukart wrote of his first time at a roller derby bout: "I know what you're thinking: women wearing revealing clothing on roller skates and beating the crap out of each other sounds like porn. But I was surprised to discover a rink filled not with size 0 blond models, but with women of all shapes and races. . . . They were there not to arouse, but to win."

The WFTDA offers statistics from its 2011 fan demographic survey that suggest fans likewise do not attend bouts for purposes of arousal. According to the survey, 66 percent of roller derby spectators are female; 42 percent are aged twenty-five to thirty-four, with another 41 percent aged thirty-five to fifty-four; 63 percent have earned a college degree, with 20 percent possessing graduate degrees; and 33 percent are employed as salaried professionals. These statistics appear to support the argument that roller derby represents a new kind of sport for a new kind of feminist. Meanwhile, other women are beginning to imagine what a fourth wave of feminism might look like. Pythia Peay mused in 2005 that a fourth wave might be "a fusion of spirituality and social justice reminiscent of the American civil rights movement and Gandhi's call for nonviolent change," and more recently there have been calls for a broader definition of feminism that would eliminate political divisions among women and include the religiously and socially conservative in its ranks. Whether the fourth wave will endorse roller derby remains to be seen.

Speculation about the nature and future of feminism is just one of the issues discussed in *Opposing Viewpoints: Feminism*. The viewpoints in this book explore major issues of concern to modern feminists and society in the following chapters: What Is the State of Feminism in the Twenty-First Century?, How Have Recent Political Contests Impacted American Feminism?, What Role Does Religion Play in Feminism?, and How Are Sexuality and Reproductive Rights Affected by Feminism? The information provided in this volume will provide insight into some recent controversies surrounding such issues as the relevance of feminism in the twenty-first century; the effect of conservative and liberal politics on feminism and women's issues; the impact of Islamic, Christian, and Jewish doctrine on women and feminism; and the role of feminism in current debates over reproductive rights, sex workers' rights, and the sexual objectification of women.

OPPOSING
VIEWPOINTS®
SERIES

CHAPTER 1

What Is the State of Feminism in the Twenty-First Century?

Chapter Preface

Women in the Western world have achieved enormous gains since the mid-twentieth century and since the 1960s in particular. And advances continue around the world. In January 2009 US president Barack Obama signed into law the Lilly Ledbetter Fair Pay Act, which amended the Civil Rights Act of 1964 to change the statute of limitations on women's ability to sue for equal pay, while in September 2011 women in Saudi Arabia earned the right to vote and run for office in municipal elections. In 2010 the *Wall Street Journal* reported that Census Bureau figures indicated that unmarried, childless women between the ages of twenty-two and thirty on average had earnings 8 percent higher than their male counterparts—a first for American women, who overall continue to earn eighty-one cents for every dollar that men make.

Nevertheless, many gender disparities exist, sometimes coming to light in unexpected ways. For example, according to the Population Reference Bureau's 2011 data sheet "The World's Women and Girls," in 2010 women made up 19 percent of parliaments worldwide. Yet some regions of the world that are typically considered unfriendly to women's rights actually have a higher percentage of female parliamentarians than regions that are thought of as having already achieved gender equality. Women make up 33 percent of parliaments in the countries of southern Africa; 22 percent in the countries of Central America; 30 percent in the countries of northern Europe; 19 percent in Southeast Asia; and just 19 percent in North America, with only 17 percent of the two houses of the United States Congress represented by women. Ellen Johnson Sirleaf, the democratically elected president of Liberia, is Africa's only female head of state, earning her post three years before the United States experienced its political "Year of the Woman"—in reference to the fact that women candidates were in serious contention for spots on both major political parties' presidential tickets—in 2008.

But, as the United Nations (UN) "Progress of the World's Women: In Pursuit of Justice 2011–2012" publication reports, although 186 UN member countries have ratified the Convention on the Elimination of All Forms of Discrimination Against Women (CEDAW), "for most of the world's women the laws that exist on paper do not always translate into equality and justice. In many contexts, in rich and poor countries alike, the infrastructure of justice—the police, the courts, and the judiciary—is failing women, which manifests itself in poor services and hostile attitudes from the very people whose duty it is to fulfill women's rights." Because of this paradox, the report says, women around the world continue to experience injustices including everything from job discrimination to early marriage to rape as a tool of war.

The debate over the current state of feminism is examined in detail in this chapter of *Opposing Viewpoints: Feminism.* The viewpoints in this chapter discuss issues such as the relevance of feminism in the twenty-first century; whether feminism provides a divisive or uniting force for women; whether the influence of conservative Christianity on feminism is favorable or unfavorable; and what role feminism should play in the promotion of larger social justice issues.

> *"We have inherited a tremendous amount from our fore-sisters to have the right to equality, to education and access to reproductive healthcare. Unfortunately our consumeristic, celebrity-fixated culture has glossed over all those things."*

Feminism Is Overlooked but Should Be Championed

Emma John

Emma John writes for the Guardian *and is deputy editor of the* Observer *magazine. In the following viewpoint, she reports on a roundtable discussion led by singer and activist Annie Lennox and including other notable women in the music and journalism industries on what feminism means in the twenty-first century. All successful and well-known in their professions, the women examine the gains that women have achieved in the United Kingdom, and the West more generally, in terms of employment and legal status, agreeing that their generation has benefited greatly from the battles waged by second wave feminists in the 1960s and 1970s. But the women also feel strongly that younger generations of women and girls are becoming victims of a "reality TV" culture in which fame and money are glorified and equality is pushed aside. Likewise, the women agree that the key to successful development in poor countries is empowering women and encouraging equality.*

As you read, consider the following questions:

1. According to Jane Shepherdson, what are the most common jobs for women in the United Kingdom?

2. Monica Ali lists some of the advances from which she has benefited, but, in her opinion, what are some of the areas in which women still have not achieved equality?

3. Annie Lennox discusses her frustration with the way she was perceived within the music industry; what does she see as an even bigger problem than being put down?

*A*nnie Lennox [AL]: Our challenge has to be: How do you create change? We have inherited a tremendous amount from our fore-sisters to have the right to *equality*, to education and access to reproductive healthcare. Unfortunately our consumeristic, celebrity-fixated culture has glossed over all those things so that we who are so resourced don't use our resources as we should. In Britain, we take what we have for granted, yet if you go to developing-world countries the disparity between men and women is enormous, and values and practices can go back to medieval times.

Beverley Knight [BK], singer: It's interesting that in the countries where women have the least power, the least equality, International Women's Day is much more treasured. Here in Britain, with our excess of everything, the very things that are so precious that the Emmeline Pankhursts gave their spirit and their lives to, we take for granted. We don't think about the struggle that other women have across the world.

VV Brown [VVB], singer and model: I'm worried for young women, how everything is about how can I be famous, how can I make money quickly? We need to make sure that our role models are not just reality TV contestants, but doctors, judges, intellectuals.

AL: There is this misconception that fame and celebrity is something to be had as a goal in itself and I'm outraged by the wastefulness of the movement of feminism, when we're just sitting on the couches, watching reality TV while our daughters are being brainwashed.

Jane Shepherdson [JS], Whistles chief executive: The majority of women in this country work in the caring professions, such as nursing, teaching, etc., and they're some of the worst-paid jobs, and a lot of those people will lose their jobs because of the coalition's cuts. Capitalism values making money above everything else. One would imagine that nurturing the next generation would be something we'd value highly. And that's something women do; whether it's because we're predisposed to it or not, women do do this.

Role Models

BK: I looked to my mum for everything, down to the fact that she wore glasses so I wanted to wear glasses. . . . As I got older it was her strength of character I wanted to emulate. What would make someone of 16 years of age get on a plane from Montego Bay to Britain and be determined to make a new life for children she hadn't even had yet? Her strength, ambition, the grace that was needed to deal with people who were hostile to her being in the country. I look at her and I still think, "Wow."

JS: My mother was a biochemist, my father a mathematician, and there was no question that one partner in the marriage wasn't as equal as the other. I came home from school and my mother was at work and if people said it was a shame I had to come home and there was no one there I thought, why? Of course my mother should work. I think that has had a huge bearing on my life.

Katharine Whitehorn [KW], journalist: And it isn't just that you say, "I want to be like *her.*" My role models were actually men. It never occurred to my father to give me a worse education than my brothers, which was a rarity in those days; and George Seddon, who I worked with when he was women's editor of the *Observer*, changed things completely by making newspapers carry pieces that women were interested in.

Monica Ali [MA], author: There was a woman prime minister when I was at secondary school, the sex discrimination act had been passed already, and when I went to college women's rights was still a politicised issue. Given all that, why have we still such a long way to go in terms of pay, boardroom inequality, lack of women MPs [members of Parliament], figures of domestic violence, percentage of housework and child care done by women. . . . Part of the answer is the tendency to blame biology. There's a tendency to shrug and say women have children so there's a career gap, instead of thinking well, in what ways can we make sure that *doesn't* disadvantage women?

JS: We kind of go, oh great, there's two women in the cabinet. That's shocking. We are half the population, we're not a minority, and we're not represented in the way we should be.

MA: Feminism has fallen off the agenda—20 years ago at college it was in our discourse.

KW: You forget how recent some of the victories are. We're taught in school that we have a right to be tried by a jury of our peers, and no woman had that until 1919 as there were no women on juries before that.

Sexism in Consumer Culture

MA: I have a daughter who's 10 and we walked past a billboard the other day advertising a TV programme. There was a row of men in suits and a woman in a thong. My daughter said, "Why is it like that? It's to sell it, isn't it?" She knows that already. I said, "Yes, it's a shame a young woman would want to be portrayed in that way," and she said, "But it's her choice, isn't it? Nobody made her do that." So how do you explain the Gramscian concept of hegemony [theory advanced by Italian philosopher Antonio Gramsci to explain why the working class identify with the ruling class] to a 10 year old? If the culture is so all pervasive that you can't think outside of it, how are you making genuine choices?

AL: This incredible consumeristic culture comes in waves in the playground, you try and resist and the trouble is you end up feeling like you are the enemy. It's everywhere, the advertising is ubiquitous.

MA: And it's dressed up in the language of empowerment of women, proclaiming our sexuality and the freedom of the individual. So if you're seen to be against that then there's something wrong with you.

BK: Annie, VV and I come from a music industry where if you dare to stick your head above the parapet and say actually I don't really want to be defined as a musician in terms of the size of my breasts, instantly marketing managers will put you in the box marked as "trouble." "She's going to be difficult."

JS: Oversensitive, irrational, all those labels. . . . I've come up through an industry with men who are quite bullying, alpha-male characters. To succeed in any business, women have to be unafraid of confrontation. But a lot of women would rather avoid it and that tends to be a reason they don't succeed as they think: "You know what, it's not really worth the trouble, I'll just do this instead."

MA: I felt great strides had been made in the literary world. After all, we all know women write. But I saw this letter in *Ms.* magazine, written to the *New Yorker*. It said: "I was already alarmed when I flipped through the 2010 December double issue that three out of the 150 pages were penned by women. Again every critic is a man and 22 out of the 23 illustrators for that issue are men." An analysis of literary journals by VIDA, which counts the number of authors' reviews in 2010, shows the average is 75% male contributions to 25% female. Women authors are not getting taken as seriously as men. It would be easy in the world I inhabit to say, there's J.K. Rowling, Hilary Mantel, look at the plaudits they get, there's no problem is there.

AL: I never thought I was going to have to struggle with issues of equality. It's not people trying to put you down, it's more about mediocrity. When they're in an organisation, people have a small vision and a blinkered idea about what it means to be an artist, or successful, and they're looking for a cookie-cutter success. When I started wearing a man's suit, I understood what I was saying—but instead people questioned my sexual orientation. The issue got reduced to one of whether I was gay. And I'm not.

BK: Certainly in music, the way people are perceived to be successful or doing well is how many "units"—not even albums—have you sold? And how can we sell this product? She's a woman: fastest way to do it S-E-X. If she doesn't have the formulaic, garden-variety look we're after she's going to be difficult. And you get women who embrace that, take that skewed image of what it is to be successful, basing it on looks, and regarding themselves as being empowered. When the Spice Girls talked about girl power, I thought, what power's that then? What are you talking about? It started the whole marketing-is-god downfall.

Advocacy for Issues of Equality and Injustice

VVB: Perceptions need to be shifted back to there being substance in things. And that comes back to education. Encouraging girls to do something that means something to them—I want to be a lawyer because I want to help someone, I want to be a musician because I love the art, I want to be a better woman because it means something to me. My mum runs a school where there are just as many female mathematicians as male ones, as many women scientists as men. Why aren't there any female producers, music engineers?

AL: There are very many other women who would identify a different type of challenge. We need to look at equality for all, not only, for example, for the 14% rise we'd like to see in salaries to close the pay gap in the UK. I had an opportunity to see the situation in South Africa, and it changed my perspective so radically once I'd understood that I am living in a bubble and the majority of women around the world do not have the access to things I have taken for granted.

KW: And it isn't just the inequality of this country with the rest of the world, it's the inequality *within* this country. We harp on about that fact that there aren't enough women in boardrooms, but for educated women in Britain we're in incredibly good shape compared to 50 years ago. And yet there are thousands of genital mutilations done in this country every year.

AL: In South Africa it's a tidal wave of HIV. I was in the offices of the *Rolling Stone* magazine at Christmas with lots of intelligent, informed writers and I asked them to put their hand up if they knew that one in three people in that country were carrying the HIV virus. No one put their hands up. You have thousands of people dying, millions of orphans and they don't know. It's incredible to me, that wake-up call I had, going into people's houses where women were dying because they couldn't get access to lifesaving medication. How do you galvanise this sense of injustice?

MA: There's a perception that as countries develop economically issues of gender and inequality will automatically get better, whereas the whole thing needs to be stood on its head so that gender inequality is at the very centre of it all. A lot of studies show that if you focus on women's rights that in itself is an engine for development. Female literacy rates strongly correlate with fertility rates, so if you educate women you will have fewer and healthier children. If you invest in women, the money they make will then be more likely to be invested in their families and local communities. Gender isn't something to be dragged along behind.

BK: To illustrate your point, when I went to Salvador to see what certain charity groups were doing to combat HIV, who was at the absolute heart of every single aspect of the fight? Women. It was the women who were educating other women, showing them pictures of different STIs [sexually transmitted infections] and saying this is what can happen if you don't insist your husbands protect themselves. I went on a march through the streets with women protesting about murders that had happened, people killed because they had HIV. These women who were seemingly without a voice were getting together, marching through the streets singing. I came home a different person. I thought, how apathetic have I been my whole life? These women are way more empowered than me.

AL: For me the anomaly is that the Western countries are so resourced. I can identify with a woman losing a child. This happened to me, I lost a baby. But I'm living in a place where I can get medical treatment. A woman in Rwanda or Uganda or Bangladesh will deliver a baby on the floor and probably it won't survive and there's a good chance the mother won't either. Being conscious of this vast disparity between our experiences, I'm appalled the word feminism has been denigrated to a place of almost ridicule and I very passionately believe the word needs to be revalued and reintroduced with power and understanding that this is a global picture. It isn't about us and them.

Putting Feminism Back on the Agenda

MA: Are you saying that despite the huge advances here we're in danger of forgetting, or not relating to, instances elsewhere?

AL: Not in danger of . . . we do. We're not even aware because it's something you can't begin to imagine. It doesn't
happen in your street.

MA: So we need to get feminism back on the agenda in
this country and one of the results of doing so will be that we
can relate back to the people and their struggle elsewhere.

AL: Katharine mentioned genital mutilation. What about
the young girl who is taken as a child bride, becomes pregnant, delivers a baby, everything is wrecked and she is inconti-
nent, and she is the victim, she is the one displaced outside
the village, [she is the one] who no one will come near. Or
the young girl in Bangladesh who is raped and then lashed to
death? These are the injustices. How can I hear this and not
do something about it?

BK: But when you speak up about it you're the one who is
labelled as combative, aggressive, because feminism is seen as
some kind of putting on of a man's angry cloak. You're either
laughed at or you're some woman with big bovver boots and
a shaved head trying to be like a guy. That's the response you
get. Feminism is neither of those two things. It's about women
caring about other women, giving a voice to those who have
no other voice.

> "We should be directing our efforts to-
> ward the millions of women who have
> never had the luxury of coping with
> the problem that has no name."

Feminism Is Irrelevant in the Twenty-First Century

Christina Hoff Sommers

*Christina Hoff Sommers is a resident fellow at the American En-
terprise Institute for Public Policy Research. In the following
viewpoint, she argues that the social and economic conditions
that led feminist pioneer Betty Friedan to publish* The Feminine
Mystique *in 1963 have changed, for the most part, to favor
women's education and employment, and American women today enjoy the best health and highest level of education in the
world. By contrast, according to Sommers, the social and economic situation for men in the twenty-first century has deterio-
rated greatly, leading men to fall far behind women in terms of
health, life expectancy, and employment participation. Yet, Sommers observes, these widespread male issues have not inspired
outrage or been turned into political causes the way women's issues have. Sommers agrees in general that women around the*

world have not as of yet achieved full equality, but she prefers ef-forts to champion the rights of women in developing countries rather than in the West.

As you read, consider the following questions:

1. According to Sommers, what is the main problem confronted by young women today?

2. Which popular humor writer does Sommers use as an example of an American housewife who rejected much of Betty Friedan's message?

3. According to Sommers, on which life factors do American women score particularly high in international surveys?

Betty Friedan's 1963 classic, *The Feminine Mystique*, opened with these words:

> It was a strange stirring, a sense of dissatisfaction, a yearning that women suffered in the middle of the twentieth century in the United States. Each suburban wife struggled with it alone. As she made the beds, shopped for groceries, matched slipcover material, ate peanut butter sandwiches with her children, chauffeured Cub Scouts and Brownies, lay beside her husband at night—she was afraid to ask even of herself the silent question—"Is this all?"

The problem Friedan described no longer exists. For most young American women today, the problem is not the futility and monotony of domestic life; it is choosing among the many paths open to them. Finding men as ambitious and well educated as they are is another challenge. Life for women may be difficult, but the system is no longer rigged against them.

In 1963, two-thirds of the American workforce was male. Most well-paid and prestigious jobs were off-limits to women. Women worked, of course, but it was the custom for many employers to think of their salaries as "pin money." Advertisers and psychologists sought to persuade women that the fulfillment of their femininity was their highest calling. Adlai Stevenson, the liberal politician and diplomat, condescendingly advised the Smith College graduating class of 1955 that it was their destiny to participate in politics solely through their roles as wives and mothers. "Women," he said, "especially educated women, have a unique opportunity to influence us, man and boy." One magazine ran an article titled "Do Women Have to Talk So Much?" Pop psychoanalysts even warned women that too much education could ruin their sex lives.

Humorless and Unforgiving

Friedan—a stocky, disheveled, volatile Jewish iconoclast from Peoria, Ill.—had no patience for such nonsense. She was given to wild overstatement, calling the suburban home a "comfortable concentration camp" where women suffer a "slow death of mind and spirit." (Friedan later regretted those remarks and apologized.) But the middle-class homemakers she was addressing tuned out her eccentric rhetoric and took away the parts of her message that suited them.

The late Erma Bombeck, a popular syndicated humorist and columnist, wrote about the night in 1963 when she and two other suburban housewives drove to Columbus, Ohio, to hear a lecture by Friedan. "This is a sexist society," shouted Friedan. "You are not using your God-given abilities to their potential." Bombeck was stunned by Friedan's harangue. She found her message too sweeping, too humorless, and too unforgiving of ordinary women. "I had a life going here. Maybe it needed work. But I had a husband and three kids whom I loved." But then Bombeck had a second thought: "I liked the part about using your God-given potential. I wondered if I had any." A few weeks later, she went to her local newspaper and asked whether she could write a humorous column about life in the suburbs.

Statistics Show Women's Advantages over Men

"The symptoms of the male malaise are already showing as men of all ages become increasingly angry, suspicious, reactionary and isolated. Men are opting out, coming apart, and falling behind," [according to Guy Garcia in his book, *The Decline of Men: How the American Male Is Tuning Out, Giving Up, and Flipping Off His Future.*] Sound melodramatic? Consider some stats: Women hold 57% of bachelor's degrees and 58% of graduate degrees. Women drive the marketplace, purchasing 83% of all goods. In 2007, they bought 53% of cars. Women hold $14 trillion in assets. Companies that employ more women than men are more profitable.

Maureen Callahan,
"Men Worry They're Falling Behind in a 'He-Cession'—
They're Right," New York Post, *July 18, 2009.*

Fast-forward to 2009, and you find that women are now fully half of the American workforce. They earn 57 percent of bachelor's degrees, 59 percent of master's degrees, and half the doctorates. Females have achieved parity with males in law school and medical school and left their male counterparts in the dust in fields like veterinary medicine and psychology. Women serve as presidents of Harvard, MIT, Princeton, the University of Pennsylvania, and many other leading research universities. Today American women are among the healthiest, freest, best-educated women in the world, and they score near the top on international surveys of happiness and life satisfaction.

No Longer the Second Sex

True, the 1970s feminist vision of a fully egalitarian society has not been fulfilled. Contemporary women and men are not pursuing identical career paths. Vast numbers of women—including many with advanced degrees—cut back or drop out of the workplace when they have children. In a 2007 Pew [Research Center] study, parents of children under 18 were asked, "What working situation would be ideal for you?" Seventy-two percent of fathers, but only 20 percent of mothers, said "full-time work." (For a majority of mothers, part-time employment was the ideal.) Hard-line feminists interpret such results as more evidence of "deeply ingrained gendering," and they work ceaselessly to reset priorities. But isn't it possible that in following the venerable feminist dream of "not being at the mercy of the world, but as builder and designer of that world," women do things their own way?

In Friedan's day, women were clearly the second sex. Not so today. Yes, many women are struggling with the challenge of combining family and work. But men do not have it easy either. They are increasingly less educated than women. They are bearing the brunt of the recession. The *New York Times* recently reported that "a full 82 percent of the job losses have befallen men." Reuters referred to the surging male unemployment rate as a "blood bath." Meanwhile, the Centers for Disease Control and Prevention's "FastStats" show that men are less likely than women to be insured—and more likely to drink, smoke, and be overweight. They also die six years earlier than women on average.

Why are there no conferences, petitions, workshops, congressional hearings, or presidential councils to help men close the education gap, the health care gap, the insurance gap, the job-loss gap, and the death gap? Because, unlike women, men do not have hundreds of men's studies departments, research institutes, policy centers, and lobby groups working tirelessly to promote their challenges as political causes.

The struggle for women's rights is far from over, but the serious battlegrounds today are in Muslim societies and in sub-Saharan Africa. In these and other parts of the developing world, most women have not yet seen so much as a ripple of freedom, let alone two major waves of liberation. We should be directing our efforts toward the millions of women who have never had the luxury of coping with the problem that has no name.

> *"We've come a long way in the past forty years; there's no 'maybe' about it. The trouble is that the journey hasn't always been in the intended direction."*

Lift and Separate: Why Is Feminism Still So Divisive?

Ariel Levy

Ariel Levy is a staff writer at the New Yorker *and author of the book* Female Chauvinist Pigs: Women and the Rise of Raunch Culture. *In the following viewpoint, she observes that much of what is believed about the history of women and feminism in the twentieth century has been falsified and mythologized, particularly the idea of bra burning, upon which so much of the cultural response to feminism has been based. According to Levy, this "false-memory syndrome" has caused feminism in particular and women in general to splinter into opposing groups that give the falsehoods an even stronger foothold while simultaneously damaging the gains that women have made and inadvertently resulting in the failure of legislation that would have improved women's lives, such as the Comprehensive Child Development Act, vetoed by President Richard Nixon in 1971. Rejection of such efforts to make working life better for American women and denial of the real victories of feminism have led to women eschewing many of the principles of feminism even while they enjoy its benefits, Levy says.*

As you read, consider the following questions:

1. According to Levy, what percentage of American women with school-age children were working as of 1960?

2. Levy takes issue with what claim made by conservative women such as Cindy McCain?

3. Which feminist organization did Betty Friedan cofound, according to Levy?

Bra burning—the most famous habit of women's libbers—caused a fair amount of consternation back in the seventies, and the smoke has lingered. Wives and mothers were torching the most intimate accessory of control; what might they put a match to next? "Often today those who cherish family life feel, even in their own homes, under constant assault," the cultural critic Michael Novak wrote in 1979. The goals of the women's liberation movement, he saw, were incompatible with the structure of the traditional family. That's why bra burning became the most durable and unsettling image of modern feminism.

So it may be worth noting that it never actually happened. In 1968, at a protest against the Miss America pageant, in Atlantic City, feminists tossed items that they felt were symbolic of women's oppression into a Freedom Trash Can: copies of *Playboy*, high-heeled shoes, corsets and girdles. Lindsy Van Gelder, a reporter for the *Post*, wrote a piece about the protest in which she compared the trash-can procession to the burning of draft cards at antiwar marches, and a myth was born. In her engaging tour d'horizon *When Everything Changed: The Amazing Journey of American Women from 1960 to the Present*,

Gail Collins quotes Van Gelder's lament: "I shudder to think that will be my epitaph—'she invented bra burning.'"

It's as if feminism were plagued by a kind of false-memory syndrome. Where we think we've been on our great womanly march forward often has less to do with the true coordinates than with our fears and desires. We tend to imagine the fifties and the early sixties, for example, as a time when most American women were housewives. "In reality, however, by 1960 there were as many women working as there had been at the peak of World War II, and the vast majority of them were married," Collins writes. Forty per cent of wives whose children were old enough to go to school had jobs. This isn't just about the haze of retrospection: back then, women saw themselves as homemakers, too. Esther Peterson, President Kennedy's assistant secretary of labor, asked a high school auditorium full of girls how many of them expected to have a "home and kids and a family." Hands shot up. Next, Peterson asked how many expected to work, and only a few errant hands were raised. Finally, she asked the girls how many of them had mothers who worked, and "all of those hands went up again," Peterson wrote in her 1995 memoir, *Restless*. Nine out of ten of the girls would end up having jobs outside the house, she explained, "but each of the girls thought that she would be that tenth girl."

There are political consequences to remembering things that never happened and forgetting things that did. If what you mainly know about modern feminism is that its proponents immolated their underwear, you might well arrive at the conclusion that feminists are "obnoxious," as Leslie Sanchez does in her new book, *You've Come a Long Way, Maybe: Sarah, Michelle, Hillary, and the Shaping of the New American Woman.* "I don't agree with the feminist agenda," Sanchez writes. "To me, the word 'feminist' epitomizes the zealots of an earlier and more disruptive time." Here's what Sanchez would prefer:

"No bra burning. No belting out Helen Reddy. Just calm concern for how women were faring in the world."

The world that Sanchez has in mind is really Washington, DC. Sanchez has a day job as a Republican political analyst; perhaps this is why she measures progress solely by the percentage of people with government jobs who wear bras. Her great hope is that there will be a female president in her lifetime, and she bitterly regrets that the former governor of Alaska did not make it to the West Wing. "Most of us *are* Sarah Palins to one degree or another," Sanchez asserts. Palin "so very clearly reflected the lifestyle choices, hard work ethic, and traditional values that so many women admire."

One sign of our cultural memory disorder is that you can describe a female governor of a state as "traditional" and not get laughed at. Conservative career women are eager to describe themselves in those terms. "I don't like labels, but, if there's a label for me, it would be 'traditional,' and I'm very proud to be traditional," Cindy McCain told voters when her husband was running for president. Since 2000, she has been the chairman of Hensley & Company, one of the largest distributors of beer in this country, with annual revenues exceeding three hundred million dollars.

Neither she nor Sarah Palin is, of course, a traditional woman. In a traditional family, a wife and mother does not pursue success outside her own home. Even when a large sector of the female population worked, as Peterson pointed out, women tried to forget this reality so that they could conceive of themselves as idealized traditional housewives. Traditionally, women were not considered suited to economic or professional independence, let alone political leadership, no matter what they had accomplished. "Billie Jean King was the winner of three Wimbledon titles in a single year and was supporting her household with the money she made from tennis," Collins writes, "but she could not get a credit card unless it was in the name of her husband, a law student with no income." Unquestioned male authority is the basis of traditional marriage, and that is why the zealots of an earlier and more disruptive time wanted to scrap it.

Feminists have long been criticized for telling women that they could have it all. But conservatives have done us one better: Apparently, you can have it all and be traditional, too. Mrs. McCain told George Stephanopoulos that she asked Palin, just after she was picked for the Republican national ticket, how Palin would reconcile her responsibilities as a mother with her prospective job. "She looked me square in the eye," Mrs. McCain recounted, "and she said, 'You know something? I'm a mother. I can do it.'" It used to be that conservatives thought motherhood disqualified women for full-time careers; now they've decided that it's a credential for higher office. All of this raises a question: Why has feminism, which managed to win so many battles—the notion of a woman with a career has become perfectly unexceptionable—remained anathema to millions of women who are the beneficiaries of its success?

Once, it was easy to say what feminism was. Its aim was to win full citizenship for women, starting with suffrage, an issue that began amassing support in the United States in the eighteen forties. More than a century later, Betty Friedan was working in that tradition when, in 1966, she co-founded the National Organization for Women, whose goal was to obtain legislative protections for women and insure employment parity. Like the suffragists, Friedan was devoted to a politics of equality.

Here's another detail we've forgotten: Historically, it was the Republican Party that was more amenable to women's rights. "It had been the Democrats, with their base in heavily Catholic urban districts and the South, who were more likely to resist anything that encouraged women's independence from the home," Collins writes. The wealthier classes, represented by Republicans, had less to fear, because their families

Protest Organizer Carol Hanisch on the Bra-Burning Myth

Women threw bras, mops, girdles, pots and pans, and *Playboy* magazines—items they called "instruments of female torture"—into a big garbage can.

"The media picked up on the bra part," Hanisch says. "I often say that if they had called us 'girdle burners,' every woman in America would have run to join us."

Nell Greenfieldboyce,
"Pageant Protest Sparked Bra-Burning Myth,"
NPR, September 5, 2008. www.npr.org.

could continue pretty much undisturbed no matter how many activities the lady of the house busied herself with: They had staff.

By the late sixties and early seventies, of course, things had changed. The argument had moved from civic equality to personal liberation: Feminists started talking about orgasms as well as ambitions. The women who marched past the Freedom Trash Can outside the Miss America pageant weren't protesting the absence of female judges; they were protesting the contest's underlying values. "The goals of liberation go beyond a simple concept of equality," Susan Brownmiller wrote in the *Times Magazine* in 1970. "NOW's emphasis on legislative change left the radicals cold." Betty Friedan became marginalized within the very organization she had started. (She was, as Brownmiller put it, "considered hopelessly bourgeois." Friedan returned fire by cautioning young women against the "bra-burning, anti-man" feminists who were supplanting her.) The radicals taking over feminism, many of whom were active in the civil rights and antiwar movements, wanted to overthrow patriarchy, which would require transforming almost every aspect of society: child rearing, entertainment, housework, academics, romance, business, art, politics, sex.

Some of that happened and some of it didn't. By the early seventies, the Supreme Court had granted legal protection to birth control and abortion. But the politics of equality—forget liberation—swiftly ran into resistance. Catholic and Protestant conservatives found a common threat: the destruction of the traditional family. The Republican Bob McDonnell, who won last week's race to become governor of Virginia, described the peril in a master's thesis he wrote in the nineteen-eighties: "A dynamic new trend of working women and feminists"—women who have sought "to increase their family income, or for some women, to break their perceived stereotypical role bonds and seek workplace equality and individual self-actualization"—is "ultimately detrimental to the family."

In the run-up to the election, McDonnell scrambled to distance himself from the thesis. But he was telling a particular truth that liberals and conservatives have different reasons for evading: If the father works and the mother works, nobody is left to watch the kids. In societies where these families constitute the majority, either government acknowledges the situation and helps provide child care (as many European countries do) or child care becomes a luxury affordable for the affluent, and a major problem for everyone else.

Social movements, like armies, define themselves by their conquests, not by their defeats. Feminism failed to make child care available to all, let alone bring about the total reconfiguration of the family that revolutionary feminists had envisaged, and that would have changed this country on a cellular level. Like so many other ideals of the sixties and seventies, the state-backed egalitarian family has gone from seeming—to both political parties—practical and inevitable to seeming utterly beyond the pale. The easier victories involved representation, or at least symbolic representation. For all the backlash against *Roe v. Wade*, the movement had steady success in getting women into the government and the private-sector workforce. The contours of mainstream feminism started to change accordingly. A politics of liberation was largely supplanted by a politics of identity.

But, if feminism becomes a politics of identity, it can safely be drained of ideology. Identity politics isn't much concerned with abstract ideals, like justice. It's a version of the old spoils system: align yourself with other members of a group—Irish, Italian, women, or whatever—and try to get a bigger slice of the resources that are being allocated. If a demand for revolution is tamed into a simple insistence on representation, then one woman is as good as another. You could have, in a sense, feminism without feminists. You could have, for example, Leslie Sanchez or Sarah Palin.

Sanchez acknowledges that Sarah Palin was a problematic candidate. She writes that Palin's interviews were "a mess," and that Palin gave Katie Couric "lackluster answers—many of which were downright incoherent." And yet she manages to wonder why female voters wouldn't "applaud her candidacy as a fellow woman?"

When Gloria Steinem wrote, in the *Los Angeles Times*, that "Palin shares nothing but a chromosome with Clinton," Sanchez was outraged. She tells us, "As I read that, it means, 'you can run, Sarah Palin, but you won't get my support because you don't believe in all the same things I believe in.'" More precisely, Palin believes in almost none of the things that Steinem believes in. But for people like Sanchez—for people who are concerned chiefly with demographic victories—that's a trivial point. Hence Palin, during her first public appearance as the Republican vice presidential nominee, could enjoin all women to vote for her: "It turns out the women of America aren't finished yet, and we can shatter that glass ceiling once and for all." Isn't that what really matters?

Revolutions are supposed to devour their young; in the case of feminism, it has been the other way around. Sanchez says that she speaks for many women who are happy to live and work in a reformed and comparatively fair America but dislike the movement responsible for this transformation. "Perhaps like me, they were put off by the brashness and tired agendas of the women's rights advocates," she writes. Content with symbolic representation, Sanchez shuns noisy activism to the point of embracing political quiescence: I am woman, hear me snore. But though Sanchez and her sisters (thirty-seven per cent of women describe themselves as conservative, and three out of four women abjure the label "feminist") may not like rowdy revolutionary posturing, we live in a country that has been reshaped by the women's movement, in which the traditional family is increasingly obsolete. As of September, according to the Bureau of Labor Statistics, more than sixty per cent of American women aged twenty and over were working or seeking work, and, according to the *Shriver Report*, women are either the primary or the co-breadwinner in two-thirds of American families. For many of them, this isn't an exercise in empowerment; it's about making a living and, for working mothers in particular, often a hard living.

Feminism as an identity politics has enjoyed real victories. It matters that women serve on the Supreme Court, that they make decisions in business, government, academia, and the media. But a preoccupation with representation suggests that feminism has lost its larger ambitions. We've come a long way in the past forty years; there's no "maybe" about it. The trouble is that the journey hasn't always been in the intended direction. These days, we can only dream about a federal program insuring that women with school-age children have affordable child care. If such a thing seems beyond the realm of possibility, though, that's another sign of our false-memory syndrome. In the early seventies, we very nearly got it.

In 1971, a bipartisan group of senators, led by Walter Mondale, came up with legislation that would have established both early-education programs and after-school care across the country. Tuition would be on a sliding scale based on a family's income bracket, and the program would be available to everyone but participation was required of no one. Both houses of Congress passed the bill.

Nobody remembers this, because, later that year, President Nixon vetoed the Comprehensive Child Development Act, declaring that it "would commit the vast moral authority of the National Government to the side of communal approaches to child rearing" and undermine "the family-centered approach." He meant "the traditional-family-centered approach," which requires women to forsake every ambition apart from motherhood.

So close. And now so far. The amazing journey of American women is easier to take pride in if you banish thoughts about the roads not taken. When you consider all those women struggling to earn a paycheck while rearing their children, and start to imagine what might have been, it's enough to make you want to burn something.

"The women's movement is now being used against us by the Christian Right, bottling their brand with the fresh new label 'female power.'"

Feminism Is Being Distorted and Destroyed by Conservative Christians

Nancy Harder

Nancy Harder is a writer, musician, and photographer. In the following viewpoint, she argues that feminism is being co-opted by the Christian political right to advance a political agenda. Harder conflates the conservative Christian tenets of wifely submission and denunciation of divorce with a media blitz advancing onetime vice presidential candidate Sarah Palin as the new face of feminism. Harder maintains that while women overall are experiencing the greatest opportunity to achieve positions of power in American history, when broken down into smaller demographic groups they are in fact still falling far behind men in terms of holding positions of power and earning money. According to Harder, the illusion of feminism's achievements has made women believe they have gained more ground than they have, and right-wing Christians such as Palin are exploiting this illusion to gain political power and introduce sweeping cultural and legislative changes.

As you read, consider the following questions:

1. According to Harder, what political issue has Sarah Palin focused on most?

2. Why does Harder consider women who call themselves conservative feminists "puppets"?

3. In what way does Harder believe women who remain silent about feminist causes do harm to others?

L ast week [in June 2010], the Southern Baptist Convention [SBC] officially denounced divorce. Their Bible-thumping decree couldn't help bring back fond memories of SBC's 1998 proclamation that "a wife is to submit herself graciously to the servant leadership of her husband."

Newsweek's front cover featured an article by Lisa Miller titled, "Saint Sarah—What Palin's Appeal to Conservative Christian Women Says About Feminism and the Future of the Religious Right."

And the *Atlantic*'s July/August cover story, by Hanna Rosin, brazenly countered "The End of Men."

Something's stirring here and it sounds a little familiar.

Women getting too powerful? Let's lay down antiquated, selective inerrant proclamations to make Rush Limbaugh–listening men and the women who love them feel better about their lives.

While we're at it, let's make a role model out of an insipid Alaskan pro-life talking head who will gladly espouse conservative, gender discriminatory doctrine under the guise of femininity and (go girls!) women's power.

Real Power

For the first time in history, women have the undeniable opportunity to be equitably powerful, to make all of our own choices in our lives and have the same opportunities as men.

According to Hanna Rosin's article, women became the majority of the workforce for the first time in US history this year.

And for every two men who get a college degree in 2010, three women will do the same.

Women live longer and are, arguably, better suited for the modern post-industrial age. According to Rosin, the attributes most desirable today, "social intelligence and open communication . . . are at a minimum, not predominately male."

Women don't even need a 1:1 ratio of men to biologically procreate—not to say anything of the complex roles of parenting.

The Gap

Despite these statistics, there is still a prevailing wage gap between men and women, one that can still be attributed to gender discrimination. As of 2006, women earned 76.6 cents to the dollar to men. African American women earned 64 cents to the dollar, and Hispanic women's earnings dropped to 52 cents per dollar earned by white men.

Not only are wages inequitable, but women continue to assume most child care and the upper echelons of society are still male dominated.

Barbara J. Berg, author of "Sexism in America: Alive, Well, and Ruining our Future" writes:

> Under then President Bush, we saw cutbacks in programs vital to women's health, reproductive rights and education. Much of this was done covertly, but when it was brought out in the open it was justified as budget-cutting for the war. The emphasis on the individual at the expense of gov-

ernment programs was also a feature of [Bush's] administration. There has been increased violence in our popular culture on the one hand, and a hyper-sexualization of women and girls on the other, in our post-9/11 society. . . . There have been reductions in child care facilities and vast food insecurities (a euphemistic term for hunger) due to wage decreases, the reduction of food stamps and the like. Something often overlooked is how many women's studies and women's history programs have been put on the chopping block because schools had to make reductions and these are among the first [programs] to go. This hurts the awareness of what is happening to women's rights.

Unfortunately, the story of how circus elephants are trained in learned helplessness resonates as I write this. When young, the elephants are attached by heavy chains to deep stakes in the ground. After ineffective struggling, the elephants give up, learning they cannot pull free. From that point on, even if the elephant has a slender rope loosely tied, it will not try to escape.

As Gavin de Becker wrote, "Because it believes it cannot, it cannot."

Don't Turn Your Back

It feels [like] the women's movement is now being used against us by the Christian Right, bottling their brand with the fresh new label "female power."

And Sarah Palin is their number one spokeswoman. God help us all.

In Lisa Miller's *Newsweek* article, Sarah Palin has become a pro-life role model, if not "prophet, ordained by God for a special role in the cosmic battle against the forces of evil."

She's giving pro-life talks to women's groups and pro-life organizations around the country. Despite other pressing issues (economy, war, oil spills . . .) abortion is still a hot issue.

Conservatives Undermine Women's Rights

For some unknown reason, Republican women support candidates and politicians who are working tirelessly to deprive women of their rights, and it is universal to all conservatives. Intelligent women would not vote for policies that are against their own self-interests or support candidates who promote corporatism and theocratic rule.

Rmuse,
"Sarah Palin and Michele Bachmann
Disgrace Women's History Month," PoliticusUSA,
March 24, 2011. www.politicususa.com.

In 2010, 11 states passed antiabortion laws and 370 antiabortion bills were introduced in state legislatures, according to the Guttmacher Institute.

Sarah Palin has even started to describe herself as a feminist (gasp! dirty word) due to her family values and devotion to her children.

Palin says old feminism is a relic of "the faculty lounge at some East Coast college."

The new feminists—the women who follow Palin—aren't third wave feminists. They aren't focused on birth control, sex [education], gender discrimination, or choosing between work and family.

According to Miller, these women, instead, seek to "submit to male authority and conservative theology while assuming more visible roles in families, churches, communities, and the world."

Staying submissive to men and conservative theology while being powerful isn't just a non sequitur. It's hollow, just like the puppets these women, who are a loudmouthed spout of men's values, end up being.

Outrage—or Lack Of

Despite the fear of the power the Christian Right have on America—the Southern Baptists are the largest Protestant denomination in the US and have 16 million members alone—the group to be worried about are the [Pat] Buchanan–coined "silent majority."

By not getting more outraged that we—women—are likely paid less, treated poorly or ignored, stripped of our ability to choose, denied medical rights and child care, and generally discriminated against while we're in the population, college, and workforce majority, we do the worst damage to feminism.

We set ourselves back, other minorities back, and the rest of the world's women back by not demanding the right to make all of our own choices and have access to equal opportunities.

So What Can We Do?

Educate ourselves about the history of women and the incredibly complex relationships between the sexes, stay aware of introduced legislation and write your congressmen/women, demand raises and equal treatment in the workforce, and support our fellow women's choices, whatever they may be.

You can also check out the Feminist Majority Foundation and the Association for Women's Rights in Development for more information about events that fight for equality around the world.

> "The failure of feminists to prop up the next generation of activists, and the focus on gender as the sole requisite for feminism, has led to a crisis of our own making."

Feminism Should Expand and Emphasize Social Justice Rather than Gender Politics

Jessica Valenti

Jessica Valenti is the award-winning founder of the website Feministing.com and has published widely on women's rights. In the following viewpoint, she contends that while feminism has long been anathema to political conservatives, the Right has been actively pursuing women's votes by positioning its female representatives as feminists. Further, argues Valenti, establishment feminism is to blame for its loss of credibility on the issue of equality because of its exclusive focus on gender, as was seen during the 2008 presidential primary, when mainstream feminism insisted that the only valid vote a progressive could make was for the female candidate, Hillary Clinton. Valenti asserts that feminist leader Gloria Steinem made the situation worse by

Jessica Valenti, "Who Stole Feminism?," *The Nation*, September 29, 2010. www.thenation.com. Copyright © 2010 by The Nation. All rights reserved. Reproduced by permission.

insisting in an opinion piece that gender was the single biggest "restricting" factor in American culture. This commitment to a single issue has allowed political conservatism to advance its own female candidates as feminists as well, Valenti explains, despite the fact that their beliefs fall largely against the interests of American women.

As you read, consider the following questions:

1. According to Valenti, why do women like Melissa Harris-Lacewell feel uncomfortable with mainstream feminism?

2. According to the viewpoint, what percentage of NARAL Pro-Choice America's organization is under the age of thirty-five?

3. How does Valenti suggest the feminist movement advance its causes in the twenty-first century?

S arah Palin opposes abortion and comprehensive sex education. While mayor of Wasilla she made sexual assault victims pay for their own rape kits. She also calls herself a feminist. Delaware GOP Senate nominee Christine O'Donnell has said that allowing women to attend military academies "cripples the readiness of our defense" and that wives should "graciously submit" to their husbands—but her website touts her "commitment to the women's movement." Pundits who once mocked women's rights activists as ugly bra burners are abuzz over the "new conservative feminism," and the Tea Party is lauding itself as a women's movement.

The Right once disparaged feminism as man hating and baby killing, but now "feminist" is the must-have label for women on the right. Whether or not this rebranding strategy actually succeeds in overcoming the GOP's anti-women reputation is unclear (see Betsy Reed, "Sex and the GOP"). After all, Republicans have long supported overturning *Roe v. Wade*, voted against family and maternity leave, and fought ground-breaking legislation like the Lilly Ledbetter Fair Pay Act. When it comes to wooing women's votes for the GOP, there's a lot of damage control to do.

The Failure of Feminists

Feminists are understandably horrified—the movement we've fought so hard for is suddenly being appropriated by the very people who are trying to dismantle it. But this co-opting hasn't happened in a vacuum; the mainstream feminist movement's instability and stalled ideology have made stealing it that much easier. The failure of feminists to prop up the next generation of activists, and the focus on gender as the sole requisite for feminism, has led to a crisis of our own making.

Conservative women have been trying to steal feminism for more than a decade—organizations like the Independent Women's Forum and Feminists for Life have long fought for anti-women policies while identifying themselves as the "real" feminists. But their "pro-woman" messaging didn't garner national attention until actual feminists paved the way for them in the 2008 presidential election. During the Democratic primary, feminist icons and leaders of mainstream women's organizations insisted that the only acceptable vote was for Hillary Clinton; female Barack Obama supporters were derided as traitors or chided for their naïveté. I even heard from women working in feminist organizations who kept mum on their vote for fear of losing their jobs. Perhaps most representative of the internal strife was a *New York Times* op-ed (and the fallout that followed) by Gloria Steinem in which the icon wrote, "Gender is probably the most restricting force in American life."

Soon after, Melissa Harris-Lacewell, an associate professor of politics and African-American studies at Princeton University, responded in a *Democracy Now!* segment, "Part of what, again, has been sort of an anxiety for African-American women feminists like myself is that we're often asked to join up with white women's feminism, but only on their own terms, as long as we sort of remain silent about the ways in which our gender, our class, our sexual identity doesn't intersect, as long as we can be quiet about those things and join onto a single agenda."

The argument was not a new one—women of color and younger feminists have often taken white second wave feminists to task for focusing on gender inequities over a more intersectional approach that also takes race, class and sexuality into account. But this intra-feminist skirmish over identity politics took on a life of its own in the aftermath of the bitter primary struggle. By pushing a vote for Clinton on the basis of her gender alone, establishment feminists not only rehashed internal grievances—they opened the door for conservatives to demand support for Palin for the very same reason. Unwittingly, the feminist argument for Clinton gave credence to the GOP's hope that the mere presence of a female on the ticket would deliver women's votes.

"New Feminism"

Is it any wonder, then, that everyone from Palin's supporters to the mainstream media was eager to paint the vice presidential candidate as a feminist? If all it took was being a woman, well, then Palin was it! The *Wall Street Journal* called it "Sarah Palin Feminism." . . .

In much the same way Obama-supporting feminists were criticized, women who didn't back Palin were swiftly denounced as hypocrites by those on the right. [Republican senator] Rick Santorum called Palin the "Clarence Thomas for feminists," blasting women who didn't support her. Janice Shaw Crouse of Concerned Women for America said, "Even feminists—who supposedly promote women's equality and the so-called 'women's rights' agenda—are questioning a female candidate's ability to get the job done." The criticism of women who failed to back Palin even indulged in sexism. [Political commentator] Dennis Miller said that women who weren't behind Palin were simply jealous of the candidate's sex life, and *Time* magazine reporter Belinda Luscombe wrote that some women had a "hatred" for Palin simply because she was "too pretty." (My favorite, however, was Kevin Burke's argument in *National Review* that women who didn't support Palin were suffering from "post-abortion symptoms.") Palin even managed to divide some feminists. Elaine Lafferty—a former editor of *Ms.* magazine who had endorsed Clinton but then signed on as a consultant to the McCain campaign—condemned feminist leaders for "sink[ing] this low" and called feminism an "exclusionary club" for not welcoming Palin with open arms.

If there was ever proof that the feminist movement needs to leave gender essentialism at the door—this is it. If powerful feminists continue to insist that gender matters above all else, the movement will become meaningless. If any woman can be a feminist simply because of her gender, then the Right will continue to use this faux feminism to advance conservative values and roll back women's rights.

A Shifting Movement

Ensuring feminism's future doesn't stop at embracing intersectionality—we must also shine a spotlight on the real feminists. Part of the reason Palin and her cohort are so successful at positioning themselves as the "new" women's movement is because we fail to push forward and support new feminists of our own. This is not to say that younger women aren't at the forefront of the movement—they certainly are. But their work is often made invisible by an older generation of feminists who prefer to believe young women are apathetic rather than admitting their movement is shifting into something they don't recognize and can't control.

For example, in an April [2010] *Newsweek* article about young people's supposed apathy over reproductive rights, NARAL Pro-Choice America president Nancy Keenan suggested that it was only the "postmenopausal militia" on the front lines of reproductive justice. Yet when I asked a NARAL spokesperson about employee demographics, I was told that people younger than 35 make up around 60 percent of the organization. And when they're not ignored, young feminists are painted as vapid and sexualized. Take feminist writer Debra Dickerson, who wrote in a 2009 *Mother Jones* article that today's feminists are all about "pole-dancing, walking around half-naked, posting drunk photos on Facebook and blogging about [their] sex lives." This insistence that a new wave doesn't exist or isn't worth paying attention to has left open the cultural space for antifeminist women like O'Donnell and Palin to swoop in and lay claim to the movement.

If the new wave of feminist—the leaders of small grassroots organizations across the country, the bloggers who are organizing hundreds of thousands of women online, the advocates for reproductive justice, racial equality and queer rights—aren't recognized as the real advocates for women, then the future of the movement will be lost.

Feminism Battles Inequities

Women vote for their interests—not their gender or age—but they still want to see themselves represented. If the only young women Americans see identified as "feminists" are those on the right, we run the risk of losing the larger cultural battle and the many younger women who are seeking an answer to the mixed messages about what feminism really is. And frankly, if we position vibrant young activists front and center, there will be no question as to who is creating the best change for women.

So instead of wringing our hands every time a new female candidate with distinctly anti-woman policies pops up, let's use it as an opportunity to reestablish what feminism is about and to support the up-and-comers in our midst. Let's focus on building power for the new wave of feminists by giving money to the organizations that best represent the future of the movement (like SAFER [Students Active for Ending Rape], NY Abortion Access Fund and Girls for Gender Equity); by providing media training and placing young activists on television and in the op-ed pages (as the great Women's Media Center does); and by pushing young feminists—not just women—to run for office.

Feminism isn't simply about being a woman in a position of power. It's battling systemic inequities; it's a social justice movement that believes sexism, racism and classism exist and interconnect, and that they should be consistently challenged. What's most important to remember as we fight back against conservative appropriation is that the battle over who "owns" the movement is not just about feminists; feminism's future affects all American women. And if we let the lie of conservative feminism stand—if real feminists don't lay claim to the movement and outline their vision for the future—all of us will suffer.

> *"Achieving gender equality is impossible
> in a framework where some of women
> are viewed as less equal."*

Feminism Should Be Replaced by an Inclusive Movement Promoting Women's Causes

Amy Siskind

*Amy Siskind is president and founder of the New Agenda. In the
following viewpoint, she maintains that feminism as it currently
exists excludes women of different ideologies and is needlessly divisive because of its focus on liberal values. Siskind argues that
the leaders of second wave feminism would have supported conservative women like Sarah Palin, Meg Whitman, and Nikki
Haley because they exemplify the values of earlier generations of
feminists, namely, the choice to work outside the home. According to Siskind, "pro-women" conservatives support women as
candidates and leaders, whereas Siskind compares more traditional feminists to "mean girl" high school cliques, refusing even
to support Hillary Clinton in her 2008 campaign for president.*

Amy Siskind, "Why the 'Pro-Women' Movement Should and Will Replace Feminism,"
The New Agenda, June 6, 2010. www.thenewagenda.net. Copyright © 2010 by The New
Agenda. All rights reserved. Reproduced by permission.

Siskind suggests that a movement that includes and represents the interests of both Republican and Democratic women is an appropriate substitute for establishment feminism in the twenty-first century.

As you read, consider the following questions:

1. According to Siskind, in what year did African American men gain the right to vote?

2. According to Siskind, what percentage of women consider themselves feminists?

3. Which female conservative media figures does Siskind mention as supporting women leaders?

Ever since Sarah Palin gave a speech to pro-life organization Susan B. Anthony List, a firestorm has erupted over whether Susan B. Anthony was pro-choice or pro-life. What we do know is that Anthony and other women suffragists battled for decades to gain the right to vote. The fruit of their labor would be the Fifteenth Amendment, granting African American men the right to vote in 1870. Of course, Anthony was buried by the time women's suffrage finally arrived 50 years later.

I, for one, would like to see a woman president (not 50 years from now) and gender equality in my lifetime.

But the current rendition of "feminism" will never get us there. The construct is divisive, proactively exclusionary and openly hostile toward women of different ideologies. Achieving gender equality is impossible in a framework where some women are viewed as less equal.

Fortunately, there is another option. A new "pro-women" movement led, initially, by women on the right. The movement is inclusive, current, and refreshingly focused on supporting women. And why should we care whether it's Republican or Democratic women (or both) who lead us to gender equality? After all, our historical women leadership is richly diverse in political beliefs and value systems.

Sadly, some current-day feminists view this ideological diversity as a death knell. When the f-word departed Sarah Palin's lips, it was officially an act of war. So shaken was the feminist center of gravity, that historical women were exhumed to be used as weapons.

And so began the battle for Susan B. Anthony. Never mind that as women historian Anna Belle Pfau points out: "These were two very different worlds. . . . Early feminists like Anthony would hardly recognize the debate that is being held today." Some feminists express righteous indignation that not only did a pro-life organization name itself after this historic woman, but also that Sarah Palin had the nerve to refer to Anthony as "one of my heroes." How utterly ridiculous! Susan B. Anthony belongs to us all, not just the 20% of women who consider themselves feminists!

Also exhumed was Betty Friedan. This time a feminist blogger asserts (without evidence) that "women such as Palin" dismiss and disparage Friedan's women's movement. Actually, Friedan, who desperately tried to make women's rights palatable to everyday women from Peoria, Illinois, would find much to like about women like Sarah Palin, Meg Whitman and Nikki Haley. These women embody the notion of having a choice: to work, to raise a family or both.

And with the benefit of choice, came women's work-life struggle: a crucial issue that has gone unaddressed. Thankfully, the pro-women movement is tackling it head-on. We should applaud Republican women for embracing their strength, power and motherhood all at the same time. Even Democratic women find it appealing: "What I like about Palin related to this whole feminist thing is that her marriage really does seem to be an equal partnership, with her husband giving her plenty of room to shine, and her not hesitating."

Gender Roles in the New Economy

What if the modern, postindustrial economy is simply more congenial to women than to men? For a long time, evolutionary psychologists have claimed that we are all imprinted with adaptive imperatives from a distant past: Men are faster and stronger and hardwired to fight for scarce resources, and that shows up now as a drive to win on Wall Street; women are programmed to find good providers and to care for their offspring, and that is manifested in more nurturing and more flexible behavior, ordaining them to domesticity. This kind of thinking frames our sense of the natural order. But what if men and women were fulfilling not biological imperatives but social roles, based on what was more efficient throughout a long era of human history? What if that era has now come to an end? More to the point, what if the economics of the new era are better suited to women?

Hanna Rosin, "The End of Men," Atlantic, *July/August 2010. www.theatlantic.com.*

We should also applaud that at a perilous time for our country, women are stepping forward to lend a hand. As [First Lady] Abigail Adams observed centuries ago: "Great necessities call out great virtues." If the fraternity of leadership is failing, it's time to give the Mama Grizzlies a chance to restore things for ourselves and our children. Even if we don't agree with the ideology of Liz Cheney, Gov. Jan Brewer or Rep. Michele Bachmann, it's refreshing and imperative to finally hear women's voices in our national discourse.

But the most exciting aspect of the new pro-women movement is women supporting women. Sarah Palin is setting the pace by not only recruiting and endorsing, but also to standing by women political leaders. And conservative women in the media like Michelle Malkin, Ann Coulter and Laura Ingraham are continually defending their women leaders.

Which is why it's so confusing.

The feminists who are now gripping onto the f-word so tightly that their knuckles turn white, do not support women. And not just women of different ideologies like Sarah Palin. Many of these same feminists did not support pro-choice, Democrat, Women's Rights Are Human Rights Hillary Clinton in her effort to become our country's first woman president. Hmmm. Let's see: Sarah Palin, who supports women, is "fake" and "shameless"; while women who do not support women are "feminists"?

As I consider "feminism" and "pro-women," here's my visceral reaction: Feminism feels like a trip back to junior high school full of mean girls—ganging up and cliques that exclude. I barely made it out alive the first time and I'm not eager to go back.

Pro-women feels mature and positive. It makes me (a pro-choice, pro–gay rights, registered Democrat) feel not only welcome, but also supported, empowered and excited. I'm proud to stand alongside conservative men who explain that they "support and admire strong, powerful, independent women." Turns out, so do I. And, yes, now I can see a path to gender equality in my lifetime.

Periodical and Internet Sources Bibliography

The following articles have been selected to supplement the diverse views presented in this chapter.

Josephine Asher	"Confessions of a Young Anti-Feminist," *The Punch*, November 29, 2010. www.thepunch.com.au.
Katrin Bennhold	"Motherhood as a Retreat from Equality," *New York Times*, August 23, 2011.
Joanna Chiu	"Young Feminists 'Rankling the Old Guard' and the Future of Feminism: A Conversation with Katha Pollitt," *Nation*, January 6, 2011.
Kira Cochrane	"'Feminism Is Not Finished,'" *Guardian*, July 23, 2010.
Lizzie Dearden	"On Campus, Feminism Wavers," *The F-Word*, August 29, 2010. www.thefword.org.uk.
G. Murphy Donovan	"Bimbo Feminism," *American Thinker*, June 17, 2011. www.americanthinker.com.
Susan Faludi	"American Electra: Feminism's Ritual Matricide," *Harper's Magazine*, October 2010.
Jonah Goldberg	"Taking Feminism Overseas," *Los Angeles Times*, March 29, 2011.
Virginia Heffernan	"The Feminist Hawks," *New York Times*, August 19, 2009.
Helen Mott	"Blunt? Stubborn? Paranoid? Don't Pigeonhole Us Feminists," *Guardian*, June 22, 2011.

CHAPTER 2

How Have Recent Political Contests Impacted American Feminism?

Chapter Preface

Hillary Rodham Clinton ran for president of the United States in the 2008 election. Once the nation's first lady when her husband Bill Clinton served two terms as president from 1992 to 2000, and then a US senator representing New York State from 2001 to 2009, Clinton hoped to earn the nomination to run on the Democratic ticket. Clinton was the first former first lady to serve in the United States Senate and the first to run for president, and in the presidential race, she won more primaries and delegates than any other female presidential candidate in American history. As author Rebecca Traister pointed out in her 2010 book *Big Girls Don't Cry: The Election That Changed Everything for American Women*, Clinton's campaign broke many barriers for women in politics; in fact, she was the first woman ever to win the New Hampshire primary.

Although her candidacy was contentious—she and the eventual Democratic candidate, Barack Obama, clashed often on issues, and the electorate was deeply divided over racial and gender issues due to the historic nature of the two candidacies—Clinton endorsed Obama in her June 2008 concession speech. Speculation among pundits ranged from assurances that Clinton and Obama disliked each other and could never work together to questions about whether he would choose her as his vice presidential running mate. Neither scenario played out when, in December 2008, Obama announced his nomination of Clinton for the job of secretary of state. She was sworn into office following Obama's inauguration in January 2009.

Clinton was not the first female secretary of state, but she was the first to play a role in a major special-operations project—the May 2011 capture and killing of al Qaeda leader and 9/11 mastermind Osama bin Laden. Although that operation was not without controversy in itself, a single photograph of Clinton, Obama, Vice President Joe Biden, and other top-level government officials, including counterterrorism director Audrey Tomason, the only other woman in the photograph, generated almost as much talk as the Navy Seal–led operation itself and revealed that a female secretary of state, no matter how hard-won her achievements, simply was not viewed in the same way as a male would have been.

The picture in question is the now iconic Situation Room photo, in which Clinton, with her hand covering her mouth, is seated between the defense secretary, Robert Gates, and the deputy national security advisor, Denis McDonough, and Tomason can be seen standing in the back. In the version of the photograph published in the Brooklyn-based ultra–Orthodox Hasidic newspaper *Der Tzitung*, neither Clinton nor Tomason appears, having been Photoshopped out. Instead, an empty chair replaced Clinton and an empty space stood in for Tomason. When a blogger at *Failed Messiah* brought the photo to media attention, an uproar ensued among American feminists, who saw the photo editing as, according to the *Daily Beast* columnist Michelle Goldberg, "literally scrub[bing] Clinton and Tomason from history." The *Washington Post* reported that editors of *Der Tzitung* explained, "Because of laws of modesty, we are not allowed to publish pictures of women, and we regret if this gives an impression of disparaging to women," causing the online feminist magazine *Jezebel* to retort, "Apparently the presence of a woman, any woman, being all womanly and sexy all over the United States' counterterrorism efforts was too much for the editors of *Der Tzitung* to handle."

The role of feminists and feminism relative to recent political contests provides the focus of this chapter of *Opposing Viewpoints: Feminism*. The viewpoints in this chapter analyze how the increasing number of prominent women candidates has affected feminism and women's rights; contemporary feminists' views on and approach to issues of race and gender; and the nature of the influence of conservative political movements such as the Tea Party on feminism.

> "I want those people who lived through the 2008 election—and in many cases suffered through it, on one end or the other—to think about the history that we all made and we all witnessed."

The Prominence of Women Candidates Has Permanently Altered American Politics and Feminism

Rebecca Traister, interviewed by Marjorie Kehe

Rebecca Traister is the author of Big Girls Don't Cry: The Election That Changed Everything for American Women. *Marjorie Kehe is the book editor of the* Christian Science Monitor. *In the following viewpoint, the two discuss Traister's book covering the role of women and sexism in the 2008 presidential primary—particularly the historical significance of Hillary Clinton's campaign. According to Traister, the election of 2008 revealed an amount of sexism still prevalent in American politics and media by which many feminists and commentators such as Traister were taken aback. Nevertheless, says Traister, awareness of the continued persistence of such sexism will ultimately improve the political process for women, who will now be able to enter political races more prepared to combat public and media fixations on their bodies and wardrobes. Traister largely credits Hillary Clinton's historic campaign for opening a path for women in politics, but she also finds that all of the women in both that presidential race and the following midterm elections were treated unfairly by male political commentators.*

As you read, consider the following questions:

1. According to Traister, who was the first woman in American history to win the New Hampshire primary?

2. What do Traister and Kehe mean by the "beauty bias"?

3. In which state did candidate Christine O'Donnell run for office, according to the viewpoint?

Rebecca Traister covers women in politics for Salon.com. Her new book, *Big Girls Don't Cry: The Election That Changed Everything for American Women*, takes us through the mixed pain and triumph of the women who made headlines in the 2008 presidential election. Recently I had a chance to talk to Traister about her book.

[Marjorie Kehe]: I'm kind of embarrassed to admit that until I read your book I didn't even think about the fact that when Hillary Clinton won the New Hampshire primary she became the first woman in history to win a US presidential primary contest. Did Hillary's story kind of get buried in the 2008 election coverage?

[Rebecca Traister]: Think about the fact that no one told you that—before me! How stunning is that?

The story of Hillary as a history maker was without a question buried during 2008. But I should qualify that and say that in part it was buried by Hillary. And we can't leave that out of the equation. Most people now are critical of Mark Penn [Clinton's campaign adviser] and I am, too. But the advice that he was giving her, which was essentially to de-sex herself, was not out of line with historic experience and expectation about how you run female candidates. What those who have run have done historically is to present themselves as tough, avoid mentioning their own femininity or selling it at all costs and this is what we saw Hillary do. And part of that meant not making a big deal about the fact that she was the first woman candidate. [That strategy] gave a lot of us permission [to] not think about the tremendous historical role that she was playing, and let me tell you, the media took advantage of that permission like nobody's business. There was no acknowledgment.

Somewhere down the line—maybe when we have our first woman president—will that be when historians will look back and say, "You know, Hillary Clinton really deserves a lot of credit"?

Without a doubt. And I think we're hearing about it now, too. The conversations we're having now about gender and politics in the midterm elections are very different from the conversations we were having during Hillary Clinton's candidacy, and even different from the ones we were having during Sarah Palin's candidacy. Many of them are dismaying in many ways, depending on how you'd like to see women depicted on the stage, and there are many troubled candidacies, but what we are seeing is the expansion of the number of models for how women can present themselves in political life. And while it can be maddening, infuriating, it is also how we're going to get toward gender equality in politics. And that is coming straight off Hillary's campaign.

I'm of the opinion that Hillary Clinton still could be our first female president. But if it's not she, it certainly will be somebody who has Hillary to thank for it.

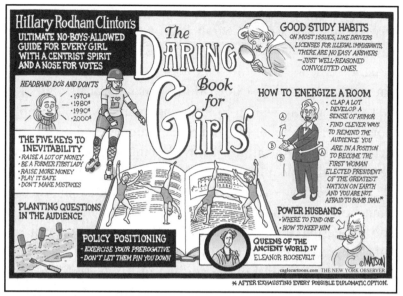

"The Daring Book for Girls" by R.J. Matson. © R.J. Matson and CagleCartoons.com. All rights reserved.

The Beauty Bias

During the 2008 campaign there were such marked differences between the way Hillary Clinton was treated and the way Sarah Palin was treated. Was that due to a beauty bias—and might it have worked the same way between two male candidates?

We would not have seen the same things at work between two men. But that's not to say that men escape an aesthetic scrutiny. We still talk about John Kennedy beating Richard Nixon in a [1960 presidential] debate because Nixon sweated his way through it. You saw John Kerry get into a flap about Botox during his 2004 campaign. You saw John Edwards get called the Prell girl for his expensive haircuts. We cannot behave as though men don't get examined for these things, too. However, we can point to the differences between the ways that these conversations take place. It's important to note that when a male candidate's looks get criticized it's often in a way that feminizes him. That's a crucial difference.

73

I was not as horrified by the fact that we were discussing what Hillary Clinton and Sarah Palin were wearing as by the way in which it was being discussed. Many people just thought, "Oh, we shouldn't talk about it at all." I understand that argument but I just don't think that it's realistic.

I was perfectly willing to have conversations, for example, about how Hillary Clinton and Sarah Palin were dressing and part of those conversations involved being critical of some of the angles that people were taking. For example, when you talk about Hillary's cackle or when Rush Limbaugh worried about how many lines were on her face or when there was a kind of jeering about the pantsuits, that's when you can say that's where the sexism comes in. [And there was] a sort of point-and-hoot festival of making fun of Sarah Palin and how much she was spending on her clothes. That kind of stuff is sexist and it's worth pointing out that it's sexist.

[But] I don't think that we should police [these conversations] to the extent that we're not having them. We should be having these conversations. It's just that these conversations are not always that fun.

Opportunity in Pain

Was the 2008 election more triumphant or painful?

If you look at the story of 2008 as its own election narrative, there was a lot more pain than there was triumph. When you're talking about women, when you look back at the sexist conversations—the conversations themselves in some ways were just agonizing. However, I am of the belief that to move forward in this country, which is the ultimate triumph, to continue to progress to a state of further inclusiveness, to something closer to racial, gender, and sexual equality, you have to work through the pain. You cannot just pat yourself on the back and tell yourself that you're over these things.

So, in a sense, the amount of pain provoked by 2008 is totally salubrious for us. Because it's forcing us to get our hands dirty in a way that we might not have chosen. We might have chosen to have taken an easier path, to have pretended that these were things of the past. But we wouldn't be getting very far if we had chosen that.

Gender Affects Perceptions

How about Christine O'Donnell? What do you think about her campaign? How is sexism at work there?

In a very complicated way. The stuff I saw the night she won the primary—which is, guys on the news pointing and laughing—I found myself so taken aback by that. I sort of wanted to say, look guys, if somebody had asked you yesterday if this woman had a chance you would have said no. And she's just proved you wrong. So why is it that you're laughing at her?

There is no question, I think, objectively speaking, that Christine O'Donnell is a terrible candidate. She is unprepared. She is not particularly engaging, experienced, or articulate on the subjects with which she is presented on the campaign trail. Her politics, to my mind, are horribly conservative, terribly conservative. There is no question that she deserves an enormous amount of criticism. However, the way her gender has had an impact on this is the national obsession with her shortcomings. Let me tell [you], around this country right now, there are lots of male candidates who are unprepared, inarticulate, inexperienced, young, and ill-suited to the jobs they are running for and we don't know any of their names. We have national cameras in Delaware, where Christine O'Donnell, who is hugely behind in the polls, is a candidate in a comparatively small state and yet she has somehow become this figurehead for women in politics.

When you look at the midterm elections, which female candidates are you excited about?

Alex Sink [Democratic candidate for governor in Florida] I feel very excited about. I think she's just a fabulous candidate. Both of these women are on the line, but Patty Murray [incumbent Democratic candidate for US senator from Washington State] and Barbara Boxer [incumbent Democratic candidate for US senator from California] are terrific candidates. And I've been very excited about Krystal Ball [Democratic candidate for Congress from Virginia]. She is 28 years old, and she has had a totally fraught campaign.

As an author, what did you most hope that readers would take away from your book?

I want those people who lived through the 2008 election—and in many cases suffered through it, on one end or the other—to think about the history that we all made and we all witnessed. I really want those of us who were pained by it or who were exhausted by it to understand the way that living through that election changed our country. Because I believe it did.

"Michele Bachmann calls herself an 'empowered' woman, but not a feminist. From where then does her empowerment come?"

Women's Rights Are Compromised When Female Candidates Reject Feminism

Lisa Solod

Lisa Solod is the creator and editor of Desire: Women Write About Wanting. *In the following viewpoint, she finds statements made by US Republican presidential candidate Michele Bachmann on being empowered but not a feminist incongruous in light of Bachmann's earlier statements that she decided to attend law school because her husband told her to and that women should be submissive to their husbands. Solod also is disturbed by Bachmann's assertion that she was called by God to run for president, wondering why God would fail to ensure women's equality. Solod insists that Bachmann would have no grounds or ability on which to run for president, or even to have attended law school, were it not for the gains made by feminists.*

As you read, consider the following questions:

1. With what prominent political couple does Solod contrast the Bachmanns?

2. What issues does Solod suggest Bachmann's god ought to take care of?

3. In what profession does Bachmann's husband work, according to Solod?

Michele Bachmann is not a feminist but she is running for president. Michele Bachmann, a congresswoman and a lawyer, is running for president. Michele Bachmann is a mother and a foster mother and a wife and she is running for president.

What part of this makes any sense at all?

Michele Bachmann, according to recent news, went to law school because her husband told her to. Bachmann is running for president, but believes that women should be submissive to their husbands.

Who then is running for president?

Is it Michele Bachmann or her husband? Who, if she is elected, will run the country? More importantly, how can we even take her seriously?

But people are. She has a growing group of supporters and a growing pile of campaign contributions.

People were furious when President Bill Clinton suggested that Hillary, his wife, would help him in his presidency. But now we have a presidential candidate who says that all her decisions are essentially made by her husband, an unsavory character if there ever was one: a man who "counsels," gay men and women out of their homosexuality. Now we have a woman candidate for the presidency who not only denounces the idea of being a feminist but defers to her husband in matters as important as her education.

Michele Bachmann calls herself an "empowered" woman, but not a feminist. From where then does her empowerment come? Were it a gift from the God she so lovingly mentions, wouldn't it have been easier for Him to just go ahead and pass the Equal Rights Amendment (which never passed). Wouldn't He have just made it simpler and easier for women to rise to the top of major corporations? How about making it a no-brainer that women would receive equal pay for equal work?

If God were in charge, wouldn't the issue of women's rights be a nonissue?

Or is God just choosing Ms. Bachmann over the millions of other women who would very much like the kind of "empowerment" Bachmann says she has? The millions of women who raise children alone, who work at minimum wage jobs, who handle the bulk of the child care and home care if they are married, the women who are abused and killed by their husbands and boyfriends, the women who are mutilated by societies who feel that women are not equal citizens: Why does He choose Ms. Bachmann over all of them? Why does God allow Bachmann empowerment and not the women of Saudi Arabia who only wish to be allowed to drive a car? Why does God allow Bachmann the "right" to run for president but doesn't interfere in selective abortion of girls?

For hundreds of years women have fought hard to be more empowered: They have marched for the vote, for birth control, for legal rights over their children. They have fought for wage equality, and justice equality. And still women fight for their rights every day: in the home, in the court, in the work place.

But Michele Bachmann can't give a nod to those who made this possible for her to be a congresswoman and a lawyer and a mother and a wife and run for president of the United States. Instead Michele Bachmann defers to her husband as the boss, and to God as her larger boss. No wonder she won't call herself a feminist.

Michele Bachmann would not be a congresswoman were it not for feminism. Michele Bachmann would not be a lawyer were it not for feminism. Michele Bachmann would not be able to juggle the demands of home and family and work were it not for feminism. Michele Bachmann would not even be able to think up becoming president were it not for feminism.

Michele Bachmann is separating herself from the hundreds of thousands of women who made it possible for her to get where she is. And finally, Michele Bachmann would not even be worth writing about and railing against were it not for the feminists who fought so long and hard before her. Isn't that ironic?

> *"This is basically a struggle over political strategy, the latest chapter in a hundred-year argument between liberal feminists . . . and left-wing feminists."*

There Is a Feminist Bias for Gender Advancement over Racial Equality

Meredith Tax

Meredith Tax is a writer, a political activist, and the president of Women's WORLD. In the following viewpoint, she reports that the 2008 primary race between Hillary Clinton and Barack Obama exposed a deep conflict within American feminism between those who posit that gender is the only issue that matters in terms of gaining equality and those who believe that gender is only part of a broader intersection of factors that include race, class, disability, and other issues. Tax examines the bitter divide evidenced by the two sides in various publications castigating either Clinton or Obama supporters for being interested only in gender or race, as well as black feminists who reasoned that their

Meredith Tax, "Barack, Hillary, and US Feminism," *Changing the Race: Racial Politics and the Election of Barack Obama*, edited by Linda Burnham and published by Applied Research Center, Fall 2009. Copyright © 2009 by Applied Research Center. All rights reserved. Reproduced by permission.

support for Obama depended not just on their gender but also on the entire history of their race in the United States. Ultimately, Tax advocates that "left-wing" feminists—who champion the intersecting rights related to gender, race, class, and other factors—must create their own movement independent of those feminists who support only gender-related issues.

As you read, consider the following questions:

1. According to Tax, what are the differences between "liberal" and "left-wing" feminists?

2. Which black feminist writer wrote of her support for Barack Obama, according to the viewpoint?

3. According to Tax, how did political conservatives respond to feminism during the 1980s?

The [Hillary Rodham] Clinton-[Barack] Obama contest for the Democratic nomination sparked more heated debate among feminists than at any time since the seventies. In rage and bewilderment, mainstream feminists asked why all women did not rally behind Hillary Clinton, while left-wing feminists wondered where they ever got the idea that they could deliver our votes on the basis of gender alone.

The primary campaign thus exposed a long-standing fault line in the US feminist movement and raised fundamental political questions. The fault line is not, as the media would have it, one of demographics—white vs. black, old vs. young, college educated vs. blue collar. Though it has racial and generational aspects, this is basically a struggle over political strategy, the latest chapter in a hundred-year argument between liberal feminists, who see women's issues as separate and self-contained, and left-wing feminists, who see them as intertwined with race, class, and other social questions.

The Clinton-Obama Debate

The debate was kicked off early in 2008 by three writers associated with the Women's Media Center: Gloria Steinem, Carol

Jenkins, and Robin Morgan. Steinem created an enormous stir with a *New York Times* op-ed of January 8, in which she responded to Hillary's loss in Ohio by saying, "Gender is probably the most restricting force in American life. . . . Black men were given the vote a half century before women of any race were allowed to mark a ballot, and generally have ascended to positions of power, from the military to the boardroom, before any women."

Frances Kissling, ex-director of Catholics for Choice, responded in *Salon:* "I do not want a feminism that is part of the status quo, and so I do not want the first woman president to be a Clintonian." Black feminist broadcast journalist Carol Jenkins riposted with a piece supporting the position that sexism trumps racism: "Gender bias cuts through race and class and age and geography with intent to undermine. And, if you're a woman of color—even more so."

The battle heated up as the New York primary approached. On Feb. 2, the Women's Media Center published "Goodbye to All That (#2)," a cry of rage by another board member, Robin Morgan, in which she accused young women who supported Obama of just wanting to please their boyfriends and went on: "How dare anyone unilaterally decide when to turn the page on history, papering over real inequities and suffering constituencies in the promise of a feel-good campaign?. . . *Goodbye to going gently into any goodnight any man prescribes for us.* We are the women who changed the reality of the United States. And though we never went away, *brace* yourselves: *we're back!*"

The next day, a large group of left-wing feminist academics, activists and writers published a widely distributed "[New York Feminists] for Peace and Barack Obama," that began, "In the coming elections, it is important to remember that war and peace are as much 'women's issues' as are health, the environment, and the achievement of educational and occupational equality." The petition went on to identify Clinton as a liberal hawk, based on her record in the Senate and her vote for the war in Iraq.

A few days later, black law professor Kimberlé Crenshaw and Eve Ensler, author of *The Vagina Monologues*, joined Hillary's critics by pointing to "the double standard" of stigmatizing Obama's black voters as racially motivated while seeing Clinton's white voters as simply voters: "At issue is a profound difference in seeing feminism as intersectional and global rather than essentialist and insular. . . . For many of us, feminism is not separate from the struggle against violence, war, racism and economic injustice."

Then a group of feminist academics, writers and activists published a petition supporting Hillary, which, after citing her "proven record," denounced misogynist attacks on her in the media: "How many women have we known—truly gifted workers, professionals, and administrators—who have been criticized for their reserve and down-to-earth way of speaking? Whose commanding style, seriousness, and get-to-work style are criticized as 'cold' and insufficiently 'likable'? These prejudices have been scandalously present in this campaign."

Patching Up Differences

Though many black feminists had yet to be heard, the struggle was heating up to the degree that a little breakfast was arranged to patch things up, according to a letter in the *Nation* written (anonymously) by black columnist Patricia Williams: "Two days after the Texas debate between Hillary Clinton and Barack Obama, a group of old friends broke out the good china for a light breakfast of strong coffee, blueberry muffins and fresh-squeezed orange juice. We were there to hash out a split that threatened our friendship and the various movements with which we are affiliated." The friends included Gloria Steinem, Beverly Guy-Sheftall, Johnnetta Cole, Laura Flanders, Kimberlé Crenshaw, Carol Jenkins, Eleanor Smeal,

Mab Segrest, Achola Pala Okeyo, Janet Dewart Bell, and Patricia Williams. A plea to unite against the Republicans followed.

But the differences were too real to be smoothed over and black feminists continued to speak up for Obama. In March, Alice Walker wrote a moving essay relating her support for his candidacy to the way she grew up as a sharecropper's daughter in the segregated South, and Linda Burnham, director of the Women of Color Resource Center, weighed in on the idea that we live in a post-racial society:

> There is a brand of feminism, amply critiqued but still very much alive, that focuses on gender bias while consistently downplaying the salience of race.... Those of us who witnessed the response to Hurricane Katrina; who check in occasionally on the racial demographics of the incarcerated; who are aware of the racial divide in income and, more significantly, wealth; who recognize that the public schools grow ever more segregated while the push-out rate for black and Latino students rises ever higher; who track the relative scarcity of African Americans in professional schools, as well as in a whole range of professions; who know that the infant mortality rate for black babies outstrips the rate for white babies by two to one; who watch the dynamics of gentrification, dislocation and homelessness—we are not convinced that racism is an insignificant remnant. And we're hard-pressed to understand why this argument should be any more tolerated when it comes from liberal feminists than when it comes from the more frankly racist right wing.

In the view of Clinton supporters like Linda Hirshman, writing in the *Washington Post*, this attitude is exactly the problem—left-wing feminists kept getting distracted by other issues instead of understanding that all women must unite in order to win: "So what keeps the movement from realizing its demographic potential?... Faced with criticism that the movement was too white and middle class, many influential feminist thinkers conceded that issues affecting mostly white middle-class women—such as the corporate glass ceiling or the high cost of day care—should not significantly concern the feminist movement. Particularly in academic circles, only issues that invoked the 'intersectionality' of many overlapping oppressions were deemed worthy. Moreover, that concern must include the whole weight of those oppressions. In other words, since racism hurts black women, feminists must fight not only racist misogyny but racism in any form; not only rape as an instrument of war, but war itself."

Burnham sees the problem differently: "For nearly forty years feminists have wrangled over how to integrate issues of race, class, sexual orientation and other markers of inequality into a coherent, powerful gender analysis. Women of color insist on the complex relationship between racism and sexism and the central significance of racism in the lives of people of color. White feminists nod their heads, 'Yes, of course, we understand, we're with you on that.' Then comes the crunch, when the content of your feminism actually matters—as it does in this campaign—and they revert to the primacy of sexism over all other forms of discrimination and oppression. All the tendencies that got feminism tagged as a white, middle-class women's thing are, brutally, back in play."

These differences about the primary were, fundamentally, a debate about basic strategic questions: What is a feminist issue? How should feminists organize? With whom should we seek alliances? Should we concentrate on big symbolic victories or work for more tangible reforms? The struggle over these questions has a long history in the women's movement.

A Brief History of the Struggle Within the US Feminist Movement

In the heyday of the suffrage movement, mainstream women's organizations adopted a strategy of concentrating single-mindedly on winning women the right to vote and were willing to do whatever it took to get white male votes, including race and immigrant baiting. The left wing of the women's

Melissa Harris-Lacewell on Gloria Steinem's Op-Ed

When [Gloria] Steinem suggests, for example, in that article [*New York Times*, January 8, 2008] that Obama is a lawyer married to another lawyer and to suggest that, for example, Hillary Clinton represents some kind of sort of breakthrough in questions of gender, I think that ignores an entire history in which white women have in fact been in the White House. They've been there as an attachment to white male patriarchal power. It's the same way that Hillary Clinton is now making a claim toward experience. It's not her experience. It's her experience married to, connected to, climbing up on white male patriarchy. This is exactly the ways in which this kind of system actually silences questions of gender that are more complicated than simply sort of putting white women in positions of power and then claiming women's issues are cared for.

Melissa Harris-Lacewell,
"Race and Gender in Presidential Politics:
A Debate Between Gloria Steinem
and Melissa Harris-Lacewell," Democracy Now!
January 14, 2008. www.democracynow.org.

movement—socialists, social feminists, sex radicals, and black women's organizations—tried to link suffrage to economic and social issues, and reached out to the labor movement and to black and immigrant male voters. World War I changed the game; when the organized left opposed US entry into the war, it was pretty well wiped out by the state. Except for the small group of militants who later formed the National Women's Party, mainstream feminists supported the war; they got the vote as a reward, but their narrow perspective and political compromises turned off the next generation to organized feminism.

A similar fault line ran through women's movement politics in the late sixties and seventies. Left-wing feminists—who identified as women's liberationists or radical feminists or socialist feminists or women of color—worked on a wide range of issues including the Vietnam war; abortion and reproductive rights; sexual freedom and gay rights; union struggles; and support for the black and other national liberation movements. But though left-wing feminists were enormously important in the beginning of the movement and in its cultural and intellectual life, they never built national organizations with broad programs that were stable enough to last. Meanwhile, mainstream feminists built strong, tightly controlled national organizations that were ideologically on message, skilled at working the media, and good at raising money. They pursued a strategy of doing everything through the Democratic Party and focused increasingly on the Equal Rights Amendment [ERA].

With the [President Ronald] Reagan era, conservatives launched a broad mobilization against women's liberation, affirmative action, gay rights, and other democratic advances of the sixties and seventies. They fought the ERA in electoral and propaganda campaigns; organized a Right to Life movement against abortion; mobilized bigotry and fundamentalism against gay rights; did extensive union busting; and undercut free expression with censorship campaigns that were thinly disguised attacks on increased sexual freedom for women and gays. Under this right-wing assault, the alliance that was the women's movement disintegrated; what remained were reproductive rights organizations and the mainstream groups in Washington. As these were forced more and more into a defensive posture, their ideas and methods of work became increasingly cautious.

The Rise of "Corporate Feminism"

Today, the organizations that are the public face of US feminism are old, bureaucratic and top-down, shaped by careerism and Washington politics. Their organizational culture is so permeated by US free market business ideology that they could be called corporate feminists: They build top-down organizations, concentrate on fund-raising, and think in terms of building their own brand and market share, not of building a broad movement. NOW [National Organization for Women], the Feminist Majority, and the National Women's Political Caucus have big budgets to meet; they need visibility to raise money, and have been utterly shaped by interaction with the state, so their perspective is always: What will help with lobbying, what will help in the next election. Their political allegiance belongs to the Democratic Party rather than to any mass base of women.

Corporate feminist campaigns tend to be narrowly constructed in gender terms, around the most middle-class vision of feminist goals—ending the glass ceiling, for instance, rather than raising the floor and giving everyone a living wage. For the most part, they avoid issues like globalization, war, or the environment, and hold back from union drives and campaigns for welfare rights. For this reason, few younger women activists—even those who consider themselves feminist—identify with the mainstream women's movement. Some of these younger feminists work in the women of color movement, in organizations like Incite!, SisterSong and the Women of Color Resource Center. Some work in labor, antiwar or anti-globalization groups, or in grassroots groups that focus on economic or race issues, though they complain that it is hard to get these groups to take up gender. Some work as junior staff in mainstream nonprofits, reproductive rights organizations, or global feminist or human rights campaigns, where they have little voice.

Though young feminists have much in common politically with left-wing feminists of the second wave, and there is informal networking and some coalition work on specific issues, mainstream organizations remain the public face of US feminism. They spin the issues their way, while everyone else plays catch-up. This is what happened in the primary debate between Clinton and Obama: While mainstream feminists went all out for Hillary—and some Obama supporters joined in sexist attacks on her—left-wing feminists tried to frame a coherent response to both without having a collective voice or national organization to serve as a platform.

Though a woman in the White House would certainly be a potent symbol and an inspiration to all our daughters, it's open to debate how much the election of Hillary Clinton as president would actually have changed things for US women. But mainstream feminists declared her candidacy the be-all and end-all of our struggle. They brought the same kind of fervor to her campaign that they had brought to the ERA in the late seventies, when they told the rest of the women's movement we should drop everything else until that got passed.

Putting all your eggs in one basket is a terrible strategy, all the more so if the basket is a largely symbolic one. A movement that has a broad program with many goals will win some and lose some. A movement that has only one object— passing a constitutional amendment or electing a particular politician—loses an awful lot when it fails to meet its goal. But the US women's movement will probably keep pursuing this strategy until left-wing feminists build our own formation capable of giving alternative leadership.

> *"Even those of us who didn't usually concern ourselves with gender-centric matters began to realize that when it comes to women, we are not post-anything."*

The Feminist Reawakening

Amanda Fortini

Amanda Fortini is a Montana-based writer who has contributed to New York, *the* New Yorker, *the* New York Times, *and* Slate, *among other publications. In the following viewpoint, she examines the need for a revived feminist movement in the wake of Hillary Clinton's 2008 run for president. Fortini maintains that apparent advances made by women in employment and education have been deceptive, and the campaign of Clinton brought the "dormant" sexism of the United States to the surface of political and social discourse. Interviewing women from a wide range of professions, Fortini finds that most have experienced either blatant or subtle forms of sexism, with some pointing out that American women for the most part want to avoid discussing the problem altogether. Fortini contends that had Clinton ad-*

Amanda Fortini, "The Feminist Reawakening: Hillary Clinton and the Fourth Wave," *New York Magazine*, April 13, 2008. Reproduced by permission. This is an abridged version of the essay that originally appeared in *New York Magazine*.

dressed the gender stereotypes she encountered during the campaign, she would only have reinforced them, making the prospect of a public forum on sexism unthinkable.

As you read, consider the following questions:

1. What does Fortini name as some of the most egregiously sexist trends in American culture?

2. According to Fortini, what is the difference between talking about race and talking about gender?

3. What is one physical characteristic that women tend to change when they enter the workforce, according to the viewpoint?

Not so long ago, it was possible for women, particularly young women, to share in the popular illusion that we were living in a postfeminist moment. There were encouraging statistics to point to: More women than men are enrolled at universities, where they typically earn higher grades; once they graduate, those who live in big cities might even receive higher salaries—at least in the early years of employment. The Speaker of the House is female, as are eight governors and 16 percent of Congress (never mind that this is 11 percent fewer than Afghanistan's parliament). Many women believed we had access to the same opportunities and experiences as men— that was the goal of the feminist movement, wasn't it?—should we choose to take advantage of them (and, increasingly, we just might not). There was, of course, the occasional gender-based slight to contend with, a comment on physical appearance, the casual office badminton played with words like *bitch* and *whore* and *slut*, but to get worked up over these things seemed pointlessly symbolic, humorless, the purview of women's-studies types. Then Hillary Clinton declared her candidacy, and the sexism in America, long lying dormant, like some feral, tranquilized animal, yawned and revealed itself. Even those of us who didn't usually concern ourselves with gender-centric matters began to realize that when it comes to women, we are not post-anything.

The egregious and by now familiar potshots are too numerous (and tiresome) to recount. A greatest-hits selection provides a measure of the misogyny: There's Republican axman Roger Stone's anti-Hillary 527 organization, Citizens United Not Timid, or CUNT. And the Facebook group Hillary Clinton: Stop Running for President and Make Me a Sandwich, which has 44,000-plus members. And the "Hillary Nutcracker" with its "stainless-steel thighs." And Clinton's Wikipedia page, which, according to the *New Republic*, is regularly vandalized with bathroom-stall slurs like "slut" and "cuntbag." And the truly horrible YouTube video of a KFC bucket that reads HILLARY MEAL DEAL: 2 FAT THIGHS, 2 SMALL BREASTS, AND A BUNCH OF LEFT WINGS. And Rush Limbaugh worrying whether the country is ready to watch a woman age in the White House (as though nearly every male politician has not emerged portly, wearied, and a grandfatherly shade of gray). And those two boors who shouted, "Iron my shirts!" from the sidelines in New Hampshire. "Ah, the remnants of sexism," Clinton replied, "alive and well." With that, she blithely shrugged off the heckling.

Sexism in the Mainstream Media

It was hardly a revelation to learn that sexism lived in the minds and hearts of right-wing crackpots and Internet nutjobs, but it was something of a surprise to discover it flourished among members of the news media. The frat boys at MSNBC portrayed Clinton as a castrating scold, with Tucker Carlson commenting, "Every time I hear Hillary Clinton speak, I involuntarily cross my legs," and Chris Matthews calling her male endorsers "castratos in the eunuch chorus." Matthews also dubbed Clinton "the grieving widow of absurdity," saying, of her presidential candidacy and senatorial seat, "She didn't win there on her merit. She won because everybody felt, 'My

God, this woman stood up under humiliation.'" While that may be partly true—Hillary's approval ratings soared in the wake of *l'affaire* Lewinsky—Matthews's take reduced her universally recognized political successes to rewards for public sympathy, as though Clinton's intelligence and long record of public service count for nothing. Would a male candidate be viewed so reductively? Many have argued that the media don't like Clinton simply because they don't like Clinton—even her devotees will admit she arrives with a complete set of overstuffed baggage—much in the same way they made up their mind about Al Gore back in 2000 and ganged up on him as a prissy, uptight know-it-all. But whatever is behind the vitriol, it has taken crudely sexist forms.

Even when the media did attempt to address the emergent sexism, the efforts were tepid, at best. After the laundry incident, *USA Today* ran the extenuating headline, "Clinton Responds to Seemingly Sexist Shouts." A handful of journalists pointed out the absurdity of the adverb. "If these comments were only 'seemingly' sexist, I wonder what, exactly, *indubitably* sexist remarks would sound like?" Meghan O'Rourke wrote on *The XX Factor*, a blog written by *Slate*'s female staffers. Many women, whatever their particular feelings about Hillary Clinton (love her, loathe her, voting for her regardless), began to feel a general sense of unease at what they were witnessing. The mask had been pulled off—or, perhaps more apt, the makeup wiped off—and the old gender wounds and scars and blemishes, rather than having healed in the past three decades, had, to the surprise of many of us, been festering all along.

Invisible Women and the Loophole Woman

Of course, we weren't delusional. Even before Tina Fey declared, "Bitch is the new black," before female outrage had been anointed a trend by the *New York Times*, many women were clued in to the numerous gender-related issues that lay, untouched and unexamined, at some subterranean level of

Most Women Do Not Opt Out, They Are Forced Out

If women are happily choosing to stay home with their babies, that's a private decision. But it's a public policy issue if most women (and men) need to work to support their families, and if the economy needs women's skills to remain competitive. It's a public policy issue if schools, jobs, and other American institutions are structured in ways that make it frustratingly difficult, and sometimes impossible, for parents to manage both their jobs and family responsibilities. . . .

Yes, maybe some women "chose" to go home. But they didn't choose the restrictions and constrictions that made their work lives impossible. They didn't choose the cultural expectation that mothers, not fathers, are responsible for their children's doctor visits, birthday parties, piano lessons, and summer schedules. And they didn't choose the bias or earnings loss that they face if they work part time or when they go back full time.

E.J. Graff,
"The Opt-Out Myth: Most Moms Have to
Work to Make Ends Meet. So Why Does the Press
Write Only About the Elite Few Who Don't?,"
Columbia Journalism Review, *vol. 45, no. 6,*
March/April 2007.

our culture: to the way women disproportionately bear the ills of our society, like poverty and lack of health care; to the relentlessly sexist fixation on the bodies of Hollywood starlets—on the vicissitudes of their weight, on the appearance and speedy disappearance of their pregnant bellies—and the deleterious influence this obsession has on teenage girls; to the way our youth-oriented culture puts older women out to graze (rendering them what Tina Brown has called, in a nod to Ralph Ellison, "invisible women"). But who wanted to complain? It was easier—and more fun—to take the Carly Fiorina approach: to shut up and compete with the boys. Who wanted to be the statistic-wielding shrew outing every instance of prejudice and injustice? Most women prefer to think of themselves as what Caroline Bird, author of *Born Female*, has called "the loophole woman"—as the exception. The success of those women is frequently cited as evidence that feminism has met its goals. But too often, the exceptional woman is also the exception that proves the rule.

Indeed, it might be said that the postfeminist outlook was a means of avoiding an unpleasant topic. "They don't want to have the discussion," a management consultant who worked at a top firm for nearly a decade told me, referring to her female colleagues. "It's like, 'I'm trying to have a level playing field here.'" Who wanted to think of gender as a divisive force, as the root of discrimination? Perhaps more relevant, who wanted to view oneself as a victim? Postfeminism was also a form of solipsism: *If it's not happening to me, it's not happening at all.* To those women succeeding in a man's world, the problems wrought by sexism often seemed to belong to other women. But as our first serious female presidential candidate came under attack, there was a collective revelation: Even if we couldn't see the proverbial glass ceiling from where we sat, it still existed—and it was not retractable.

Politicized and Re-Politicized Women

The women I interviewed who described a kind of conversion experience brought about by Clinton's candidacy were professionals in their thirties, forties, and fifties, and a few in their twenties. In some cases, the campaign had politicized them: Women who had never thought much about sexual politics were forwarding Gloria Steinem's now infamous op-ed around, reiterating her claim that "gender is probably the most restricting force in American life." In other cases, it had *re-*

politicized them: A few women told me they were thinking about issues they hadn't considered in any serious way since college, where women's studies courses and gender theory were mainstays of their liberal arts curricula. "That whole cynical part of me that has been coming to this conclusion all along was like, I knew it! We've come—not nowhere, but not as far as we thought," one said. A not insignificant number of women mentioned arguments they'd had with male friends and colleagues, who disagreed that Clinton was being treated with any bias. A high-powered film executive for a company based in New York and Los Angeles recounted a heated debate she engaged in with two of her closest male friends; she finally capitulated when they teamed up and began to shout her down. Nearly all of the women I interviewed, with the exception of those who write on gender issues professionally, refused to be named for fear of offending the male bosses and colleagues and friends they'd tangled with.

In particular, the campaign has divided women and the men they know on the subject of race. Indelicate as it seems to bring up, the oft-repeated question is, why do overtly sexist remarks slip by almost without comment, while any racially motivated insult would be widely censured? A few women told me that when they raised this issue with men, the discussion broke down, with the men arguing that racism was far more pernicious than sexism. "If you say anything about the specificity of Hillary being a woman, you're just doing the knee-jerk feminist stuff, that's the reaction," said one woman who asked not to be identified in any way. "Thinking about race is a serious issue, whereas sexism is just something for dumb feminists to think about." The point is not to determine whether it is harder to be a white woman or a black man in America today, nor which candidate would have more symbolic value. At issue is the fact that race is, as it should be, taboo grounds for criticism, but gender remains open territory.

The Sexual Politics of Dress and Demeanor

In the public realm, women are frequently subjected to a sort of bodily lit-crit, where dress and demeanor are read as symbolic of femininity or a lack thereof. We have seen this with Hillary: Her current pantsuits, her erstwhile headbands, that sliver of cleavage, have all generated much speculation. Geraldine Ferraro told me that the scrutiny hasn't changed all that much from a quarter century ago. "When I ran for VP, they said, 'You have to wear a jacket'—I was going to wear a short-sleeved dress. They said, 'We haven't seen that with a VP candidate before,' and I said, 'I don't care, you haven't seen a woman candidate before.'" Professional women, too, experience a version of this and tend to be acutely aware of the assumptions that can arise from their choices. Do you wear the glasses to the interview, or take them off? Button up the jacket, or leave it open? Pull the hair up, or leave it down? Allow a hint of sexiness to wink at the male interviewer or recruiter or boss, or go the androgynous route? For women in clubby, male-dominated industries, like banking and consulting, the objective is often to appear more masculine (and ward off the suspicion that you will someday procreate and thus become professionally unviable). "They cultivate a hard edge, pressing to be more masculine in their manner and the way they deal with people," the management consultant told me. "They develop a reputation for being cutthroat, for being hard, even harder than men, for having exacting standards. If I think of the women I know who have gone into banking, their personalities have changed; there's a difference in their whole bearing."

But some intrinsically female characteristics are more complicated to manipulate. One's voice, for instance: Clinton's flat, nasal, and, lately, hoarse voice has not fared well against Obama's rich baritone. The pundits have repeatedly labeled her shrill—another criticism that is only ever made of a woman. The sound of a woman's voice is among the most important factors determining her success. Margaret Thatcher famously lowered her pitch on the advice of a spin doctor, and she's not the only one. A study that compared female voices between 1945 and 1993 found that, in the latter half of the century, as young women entered the workforce in increasing numbers, their voices deepened, with the average pitch decreasing about 23 hertz. Think of that "career-woman voice" donned, consciously or not, by so many working women in Manhattan. A high, reedy, or uncertain voice can stall a woman's ascent. When my former (female) boss told me I needed to work on "presentational confidence," I concentrated on making my voice, and speech, more commanding.

Persistent Stereotypes

Another way women attempt to transcend stereotypes is through what Linda Hirshman calls "the dancing backwards in high heels thing"—or, working harder than any man presumably would. Nearly all the women I spoke to referred to the feeling that one can confound perceived gender limitations by doing a more thorough job, being smarter, better informed, better researched. I think of it as the studying-for-extra-credit approach. The idea is that we can shift the focus from the arbitrary, personal criteria by which we are evaluated—whether we have children or not, are married or not, are warm enough, or too cold, or too calculating, or overly ambitious—onto our achievements. But it doesn't necessarily happen that way, as many of us, including Hillary Clinton, have learned. It turns out that even the tendency to over-prepare is gendered (to borrow a term from the women's-studies crowd) in the popular perception. Clinton is portrayed as a Tracy Flick [a fictional character in the novel *Election*] type, as one of those girls: the ones actually studying in study hall. In real life, that gets you elected class secretary or VP of operations, but never the No. 1 spot. "Leadership" is more effortless, an *assumed* mantle of authority, confidence that doesn't need a PowerPoint presentation to back it up. But it's difficult to imagine this traditionally male archetype—embodied in Obama's easy manner and unscripted, often overly general approach—working for a woman in the same way it does for a man. "There's no way you could put his words, his message, in her mouth and get away with it," said one of the women I spoke with. "If you took his campaign message, his speeches, his everything and you put it on her, she'd be f--- ed."

None of this is to say Obama hasn't had his own stereotypes to confront during this campaign. He has faced criticism for being "too black" or "not black enough." He's had to battle the unfounded yet persistent Internet rumor that he's a radical Muslim. And when his controversial pastor evoked questions about race and patriotism, Obama promptly dealt with the matter, giving one of the most complex and sophisticated speeches a politician has ever delivered.

There has been clamoring for Clinton to make the gender equivalent of Obama's race speech. In this idealized homily, Clinton would confront the insidiousness of sexism and speak out against the societal ills that affect women; she would renounce the unfair criteria, at once more stringent and more superficial, by which women are judged. She might even address the compromises she is said to have made in her life— this is idealized, remember—and tell us why those compromises, rather than making her an inferior candidate, instead make her a stronger one, as they can be viewed as her imperfect resolutions to the dilemmas faced by many women: Do you stay with a man who has betrayed you, or divorce him? Do you keep your name, or take your husband's? Do you put your career aside for his—at least for a time?

This speech, of course, is not likely to happen. Not only because, as was pointed out on *The XX Factor*, women disagree on such fundamental issues as abortion and child care, or because Clinton is politically cautious and to do so would risk alienating male voters. A speech like this would open Clinton to the criticism, leveled at her several times already in this campaign, and at any female candidate who refers to her gender or acts in a particularly feminine way (by crying, for instance)—that she is "playing the gender card." It would also, sadly, only serve to reinforce the sort of stereotypes she would hope to counter: the nag, the crusading feminist, the ball-buster, the know-it-all with reams of statistics at the ready. But the fact that women are even imagining what such a speech would sound like on the national stage is significant.

> *"If the Tea Party has any legitimate national leadership, it is dominated by women."*

The Tea Party's Alternative Brand of Feminism Engages Women

Hanna Rosin

Hanna Rosin is a writer and a contributing editor at the Atlantic. In the following viewpoint, she examines the Tea Party as a more viable political option for women than the two major parties, which are largely dominated by men. The Tea Party, Rosin finds, appeals to women who have never considered themselves feminists but who would like to become more involved in the political process. Christian conservatives in particular, according to Rosin, are apt to be comfortable with an increased role for women in positions of leadership, modeled at least in part on Sarah Palin's public persona as a successfully managing mother and political voice. Alienation from both major political parties plays a role in why so many women are attracted to the Tea Party, says Rosin, comparing the Tea Party women to the role played by Dolly Parton in the movie 9 to 5.

As you read, consider the following questions:

1. According to Rosin, what percentage of Tea Party activists are women?

2. How many Tea Party state coordinators are women, according to Rosin?

3. What does Rosin say some Tea Party women think about issues such as abortion?

In a different political season, Lou Ann Zelenik would be too much an outsider to run for a congressional seat in Tennessee. A single mother, she owned a heavy construction company until she retired in 2007. She likes to remind people that she's a "licensed blaster," which refers both to her technical skills and her Rosie the Riveter attitude. "She's bucked every trend, and if there's ever an obstacle put in her way she breaks right through it," says her spokesman, Jay Heine. Zelenik only really broke through in electoral politics, however, when she got involved with the local Tea Party. She put together a rally in Murfreesboro, and 3,000 people showed up. She hooked into a network of activist local moms who agreed to volunteer on her campaign. "A lot of the Tea Party women are inspired by seeing a strong woman run for office," adds Heine.

Is the Tea Party a women's movement? More women than men belong—55 percent, according to the latest Quinnipiac [University] poll. And while no movement that uses Michelle Malkin as a poster girl could fairly be described as feminist, the party has become an insta-network for ambitious women like Zelenik. Some are aspiring candidates who could never get traction within the tight, local Republican Party networks. Some are angry-mom-activist types who, like their heroine Sarah Palin, outgrew the PTA. But some would surprise you with their straightforward feminist rage. For the last few years Anna Barone, a Tea Party leader from Mount Vernon, N.Y., has used the e-mail handle annaforhillary.com: "The way they treated Hillary is unforgiveable, and then they did it to Sarah Palin," she said. "I've been to 15 Tea Party meetings and never heard a woman called a name just because she's powerful. I guess you could say the Tea Party is where I truly became a feminist."

A Feminist Cooperative?

If the Tea Party has any legitimate national leadership, it is dominated by women. Of the eight board members of the Tea Party Patriots who serve as national coordinators for the movement, six are women. Fifteen of the 25 state coordinators are women. One of the three main sponsors of the Tax Day Tea Party that launched the movement is a group called Smart Girl Politics. The site started out as a mommy blog and has turned into a mobilizing campaign that trains future activists and candidates. Despite its explosive growth over the last year, it is still operated like a feminist cooperative, with three stay-at-home moms taking turns raising babies and answering e-mails and phone calls. Spokeswoman Rebecca Wales describes it as a group made up of "a lot of mama bears worried about their families." The Tea Party, she says, is a natural home for women because "for a long time people have seen the parties as good-ole-boy, male-run institutions. In the Tea Party, women have finally found their voice."

Some of Wales's mama bears are the heirs of old-timey political movements like the temperance movement, which women led as keepers of moral purity and domestic harmony. Their more immediate inspiration is the conservative-mom revolution of the mid-1990s. During the [Newt] Gingrich revolution, a crew of evangelical moms came in, vowing to protect traditional family values. At that time, there was still some ambivalence among conservatives about women abandoning their domestic duties to run for public office. I recall back then interviewing Vern Smith, husband of Linda Smith, then a new Republican congresswoman from Washington. "It's funny, with Linda away, we end up sacrificing some of that traditional family life to pass some of that heritage to our children," he told me.

Now that ambivalence is mostly gone. The conservative woman in public office or otherwise working too hard is an accepted breed. Her rise was accelerated by the recession, which pushed millions more women into the workforce, sometimes as the family's only breadwinner. The stay-at-home mom is a vanishing type anyway; only one in five families has a working father and stay-at-home mother. And then there's Sarah Palin, who created a whole new model of mother activist. None of the contradictions got worked out: she works; she has small children; she defends the traditional family although she's probably home only one day a week. Never mind, after 20 years, conservatives have made peace with her type, and embraced it.

Women Balancing Budgets

And so the conservative mama bear has become a fully operational, effective political archetype. She is mother as übercompetent CEO, monitoring with vigilance her own family bank account, the local school bank account, and, as a natural extension, the nation's. "Women are sitting at home and balancing their checkbook, leaving money for groceries and utilities and fun stuff," says Jenny Beth Martin, one of the Patriots' national coordinators. "They realize that these things that apply to their household budgets also apply to government." In explaining their view on the stimulus money, several Tea Party mama bears used examples they'd heard at PTA meetings. Why should the school waste money on a part-time Chinese teacher who gets full benefits? Why should the government waste money on ant farms and exotic fish?

Christen Varley is the president of the Boston Tea Party. Last year, her husband spent some time without a job. And so, after 11 years of staying home with their daughter, Varley got part-time work at a nonprofit. She also got involved in local politics and, last year, started a Tea Party branch. At the meetings, equal numbers of men and women show up. But women end up being more dedicated. They write the newsletters and put together the database. When the group first put together the steering committee, it had four men and two women. "We ought to have a few more women," she thought, so she added some. "We're more likely to get fired up," she says. "Women take it personally. These are my *kids* they're coming after."

Mostly what Varley likes is that the movement feels like an actual tea party. She used to go to Republican town committee meetings, but except for the annual Christmas party, it was all "work, work, work." At Tea Party meetings, the women "get together and commiserate, and cheerlead each other. When the media and the culture demonize us, we feel good that there are other people just like us. We're building a lot of friendships."

Uniting Against the Major Parties

The mama bears are not the only type of women in the movement. Local parties in Seattle, New York, and California, for example, breed more-straightforward feminists. (Remember annaforhillary.com.) Some of the women I interviewed are longtime women's activists who feel alienated from both parties and are happy to have a fresh start. Betty Jean Kling runs a group called Majority United, dedicated to getting more women in office and fighting violence against women. Like many activists I talked to, Kling thinks social issues such as abortion are just wedges to drive women apart. (Varley, who is Catholic and pro-life, said the same thing: "We would be stupid to bring up abortion at a meeting.")

Kling says the two parties "just throw crumbs to women" and insult them. She has given over her radio show to women Tea Party activists and candidates, and started a network of local chapters. "Each woman has her reasons for joining," she says, "but I would like to believe that deep down she has a degree of pride in knowing that when she is voting out the incumbents she may be voting in a new woman with new ideas who will be really amenable to women's rights."

Like other Tea Party ideologies, the movement's feminist streak is not always consistent or coherent. But affiliated women candidates take away a unifying narrative that taps into both traditionalism and feminist rage. It's the feminism of the 1980 Dolly Parton movie *9 to 5*, part anger against the good ole boys and part "leave me alone." Candidate Liz Carter complains about the lack of women in any congressional seats in Georgia. FOX analyst Angela McGlowan, running for Congress in Mississippi, calls herself a "warrior." Christine O'Donnell, running for Senate in Delaware, claims she's an antidote to the "lords of the back room." *Lords of the back room.* There's a phrase Germaine Greer [a feminist activist] would like.

| "Conservative feminism in the US is hardly new."

Conservative Feminists' Impact on American Politics Is Questionable

Sophie Elmhirst

Sophie Elmhirst is a contributing writer to the New Statesman. *In the following viewpoint, she considers the emergence of conservative feminism as a force in American politics. Elmhirst focuses on the strong motherly role many Tea Party conservative feminists fill. Elmhirst describes how many Tea Party women feel the need to correct the liberal association with the term "feminism."*

As you read, consider the following questions:

1. According to the viewpoint, how many Tea Party supporters are female?

2. As stated in the viewpoint, what is the "List"?

3. What was one of the early "incarnations" of conservative feminism in the United States?

In Douglas County, Colorado, lives Lu Busse—mother, grandmother, activist and the original "mama grizzly". Long before Sarah Palin conjured up the image of a mother bear "that rises up on its hind legs when somebody's coming to attack their cubs", Busse had been calling herself "Grizzly Granny Lu" on her blog. "I always said that if we give up on the Republican Party and start a new party, we're going to be the Grizzly Bears," she tells me. "These donkeys and elephants, that's ridiculous. In America, if you're not a grizzly bear, you're not really American."

Busse founded her local 9/12 Project group in April last year [2009], just a month after the FOX News presenter Glenn Beck launched the national project based on nine principles and 12 values (numbers one and two: "America is good" and "I believe in God and He is the center of my life"). Busse now chairs the statewide coalition of 9/12 groups, and works closely with the Tea Party movement. Locally, female membership is dominant; Busse says that around 60 per cent of the activists she works with are women. It mirrors the national picture. A poll conducted by Quinnipiac University in March this year suggested that 55 per cent of Tea Party supporters are female. And they are growing in power. In the past few months, a string of ultra-conservative female candidates, such as Christine O'Donnell in Delaware and Kristi Noem in South Dakota, have won in the Republican primary elections.

Palin calls it a "mom awakening", a movement of newly empowered conservative women who are anti-government, anti-establishment and seeking to destabilise a political system they perceive as elitist and remote. The appeal of candidates such as O'Donnell is their lack of political experience: They are traditional, homely mothers. Yet the ambition of activists such as Busse is huge. She wants to change "the whole direction of the way the country's moving"—and believes she can.

When I ask her if she feels part of a women's movement, Busse reflects for a moment, and then says: "It's not a women's

History Cannot Predict the Future of Conservative Feminism

For good or ill, Christian women have moved mountains before in the American past. The abolition of slavery and the prohibition of liquor are just two examples. Now they have helped organize the Tea Party and their new conservative feminism may just affect American political culture in unpredictable ways. Perhaps they will gain a new self-confidence and political influence by straying from the Republican Party. Or, as in the past, they may disappear into their homes and churches and become a footnote in the history of American politics. For now, it is too soon to tell how the Tea Party, let alone its female members, will fare in the future.

Ruth Rosen,
"The Tea Party and the New Right-Wing Christian Feminism,"
openDemocracy.net, July 5, 2010. www.opendemocracy.net.

movement in a way that the movement that generated feminism is. This is a movement that wants our country to be the country we grew up in—we want that for our children and our grandchildren. So it gets to our motherly instincts. It's not about women's issues."

Conservative Feminism

It is a telling distinction. For Busse and others like her, feminism is a word laden with alien liberal values, wedded to a time of sexual liberation and immorality. Instead, their bond is motherhood, as reflected in an expanding behind-the-scenes network of activist organisations: As a Mom; Concerned Women for America; Moms for Ohio; Homemakers for America; American Mothers.

Palin gave her "mama grizzly" speech at a breakfast meeting of the Susan B. Anthony List in May this year [2010]. Founded in 1992 and named after the 19th-century civil rights leader who campaigned for women's suffrage, the List works like an engine room behind conservative female candidates, providing financial backing and mobilising supporters. With 280,000 members, it has funded and campaigned for O'Donnell, Noem and about 25 other candidates across the US. It also has one specific aim, says the group's chair, Marjorie Dannenfelser, which is to "help elect and involve pro-life women in the political project": to end the practice of abortion.

"What we're seeing," Dannenfelser tells me, "is a correction of the term feminist, an editing—women who feel very strongly about the talents and skills and power of women, but who don't feel that abortion is an avenue to that." For Kathleen Blee, a professor of sociology at [the University of] Pittsburgh, the idea that women such as Dannenfelser describe themselves as feminists is extraordinary. "It's a terrible distortion," she says. "It strips most of the meaning away from feminism. . . . They don't support equal rights, they don't support abortion—you name the feminist issues, they are on the other side." Dannenfelser says that the election races she gets most excited about are those featuring "women running against women where there's a clear contrast between the type of feminism the two candidates represent"; as in, one is pro-life, the other pro-choice. It's a strange kind of sisterhood.

History of Conservative Feminism

Conservative feminism in the US is hardly new. One of its early incarnations was the Woman's Christian Temperance Union, established in 1880 as part of the temperance movement campaigning for the prohibition of alcohol (a movement in which Susan B. Anthony was heavily involved). According to Blee, early rightist women's activism often had a racist tendency. Those involved in the pro-suffrage movement, for example, were galvanised to ensure that white female voters could outnumber black men. A number of those women, Blee says, became an influential presence in the Ku Klux Klan, whose membership included at least half a million women at its peak in the 1920s. . . .

The Tea Party has proved to be a magnet to the Christian right, and has been infused by the movement's socially conservative values, even though its original objectives were exclusively fiscal. (Busse is typical in citing the bailout of the banks after the 2008 financial crisis as the trigger for her activism.) For Tea Party purists, the infiltration by Christian groups is not necessarily welcome. One activist I spoke to felt their preoccupation with moral issues was potentially divisive, and diluted the Tea Party's central messages around tax and spending. But Dannenfelser sees it differently. "There is so much overlap in the Tea Party movement between economic and social issues that there is really no discontent," she says. "It is simply a matter of emphasis." . . .

Since the Tea Party rose up across the US in 2009, a common response to its more extreme factions and candidates has been amusement. Conservative female politicians such as O'Donnell are routinely dismissed, even by leading figures within the Republican Party. Karl Rove recently described O'Donnell's rhetoric as "nutty". Yet the mass appeal of these women is already translating into votes and victories. To discount them is to underestimate their growing power, and also makes for ineffective opposition. As Blee says: "People here do not take women very seriously, they do not take the Tea Party as a whole very seriously, and I think it's clear that's a mistake."

Periodical and Internet Sources Bibliography

The following articles have been selected to supplement the diverse views presented in this chapter.

Madeleine Bunting	"Clinton Is Proving That a Feminist Foreign Policy Is Possible—and Works," *Guardian*, January 16, 2011.
Mary Kate Cary	"The New Conservative Feminist Movement," *U.S. News & World Report*, June 23, 2010.
Angela Cummine	"Should Feminists Back Michele Bachmann?," *Guardian*, August 25, 2011.
Kay S. Hymowitz	"Sarah Palin and the Battle for Feminism," *City Journal*, Winter 2011.
Danielle Kurtzleben	"Sarah Palin, Hillary Clinton, Michelle Obama, and Women in Politics," *U.S. News & World Report*, September 30, 2010.
Kathryn Jean Lopez	"Forget You, Feminism," *National Review Online*, July 4, 2011. www.nationalreview.com.
Robert Stacy McCain	"Fierce, Anti-Feminist, and In Your Face," *American Spectator*, April 4, 2011.
Anne Perkins	"Feminism in Politics Needs to Be Serious," *Guardian*, April 28, 2010.
Kirsten Powers	"Michele Bachmann: Don't Call Her a Feminist," *Daily Beast*, June 28, 2011. www.dailybeast.com.
Naomi Wolf	"America's Reactionary Feminists," Project Syndicate, August 1, 2011. www.project -syndicate.org.

OPPOSING
VIEWPOINTS®
SERIES

CHAPTER 3

What Role Does Religion Play in Feminism?

Chapter Preface

One of the most vocal opponents of the way Islam affects women is also one of the most controversial figures in contemporary feminism. Ayaan Hirsi Ali was born in Mogadishu, Somalia, in 1969. Her family lived for short periods in Saudi Arabia and Ethiopia before moving to Kenya, from which Hirsi Ali sought asylum in the Netherlands in 1992, citing her objections to an arranged marriage. It has since come to light that Hirsi Ali gave a false name and birth date on her appeal for asylum, and others have claimed that her story of fleeing an arranged marriage to a distant cousin is also untrue. Hirsi Ali had been a devout Muslim in her early years. Against her father's wishes, her grandmother had the excruciatingly painful and deeply controversial practice of female genital mutilation (FGM) performed on Hirsi Ali when she was just five years old. Yet she voluntarily wore a hijab as a schoolgirl and practiced Islam.

Nevertheless, after studying at Leiden University in the Netherlands and following the terrorist attacks on the United States on September 11, 2001, Hirsi Ali has attested that she experienced a crisis of belief. In 2002, she has stated, she became completely disillusioned with religion and announced that she had become an atheist. Over the next year she focused on abuses of women and girls under Islam and, in 2003, was elected to Dutch parliament running on a platform that focused strongly on that issue. During her time in office, Hirsi Ali became increasingly critical of Islam, culminating in her involvement in the production of a film by Dutch filmmaker Theo van Gogh in 2004. The eleven-minute film, *Submission*, was written by Hirsi Ali, who also narrated. It featured an actress wearing a sheer full-length veil with passages from the Quran that typically are used to justify practices such as honor killing, wife beating, and denying girls an education written on her naked body. The film was shown on the Dutch public television network and immediately inflamed the Netherlands' considerably large Muslim immigrant community. In November 2004 van Gogh was murdered on a street in Amsterdam by a Muslim extremist, who attached a note to his body with a knife threatening Hirsi Ali's life as well.

Hirsi Ali went into hiding. The Dutch government provided her with security guards and a safe house, but neighbors eventually complained that they could not live normally in that situation. Hirsi Ali was moved, and a private fund was set up to pay for her protection. More controversy followed, however, when it was discovered that she had possibly lied on her application for refugee status. Hirsi Ali admitted to lying but maintained that the true information was public knowledge because she had published it in an earlier book. Another allegation, that she was not in immediate danger of submitting to a forced marriage, came to light as well. She resigned her post in 2006 but retained a Dutch residency permit and citizenship, although she later claimed she had admitted to lying under duress. Arguments over her situation among Dutch parliamentarians were so heated that in June 2006 the country's parliament fell into total disarray and dissolved.

Hirsi Ali was granted a visa by the United States, where she moved in 2006. She joined the American Enterprise Institute for Public Policy Research, known as a strongly conservative think tank. This raised questions about Hirsi Ali's political and religious allegiances since she had formerly been a member of a center-left political party in the Netherlands. In 2010 Hirsi Ali published a book of memoirs, *Nomad: From Islam to America—A Personal Journey Through the Clash of Civilizations*, in which she again courted controversy by suggesting that liberal reform Christians should actively try to convert Muslims to Christianity.

The positive and negative effects of religion on feminism and women's rights is analyzed in this chapter of *Opposing Viewpoints: Feminism*. The viewpoints in this chapter present a variety of perspectives on such issues as the relationship between Islam and feminism and between Western feminists and Middle Eastern women living under Islamic Law; the effects of Christian dogma on gender equality, social justice, and society's roles for men and women; and the extent to which feminism can or cannot be reconciled with Judaic doctrine and traditional roles for women.

> *"In every Muslim context, minority or majority, in every class from the very poor or basic to the very wealthy and affluent, Muslim women are active in the promotion of their own well-being."*

Islamic Feminism Promotes Gender Equality and Religious Identity

Amina Wadud

Amina Wadud is an American-born professor emeritus of Islamic studies at Virginia Commonwealth University, is the author of numerous works on women and Islam, and has conducted coed prayer services as an imam. In the following viewpoint, she explains that practicing Islam is a fundamental element of most Muslim women's identities and argues that there is no need for them to choose between their faith and their rights. According to Wadud, Westerners generally know about Muslim women's lives only through what they are told by non-Muslims or those who have become alienated from Islam, and therefore the view is skewed. Wadud asserts that the core tenets of Islam dictate justice both in society and within the home, in-

cluding gender equality, and that Muslim women can approach feminism through the lens of Islam to advocate for their rights. According to Wadud, Muslim women must remove Islam from its current patriarchal context and instead return to its central message.

As you read, consider the following questions:

1. What reason does Wadud give for her early rejection of the term "feminist"?

2. How does Wadud explain "secular" Islam?

3. What does Wadud say are the "primary sources" of Islam in addition to the Quran?

Well, I suppose I can't go on avoiding the white elephant in the room, even if it is purple.

This week [in September 2010] a young feminist Muslim from Egypt is visiting in the Bay Area under a program from the US Department of State, called an "exchange." But they don't exchange, she said, they only tell us and tell us and tell us—as if Muslim women are clean slates that need to be informed by the likes of the State Department. But it's not just my young friend, but other fabulous Muslim women from Bahrain, Saudi Arabia, and Morocco. I am still surprised how much the image of the oppressed Muslim woman as victim remains credible. Here is where I enter, but it will take me more than 1500 to 2000 words, so I'll be back, you can count on it.

Let me start with the definition of feminism that I am most comfortable with: Feminism is the radical idea that women are human beings. Then, let me add the most comfortable definition of Islam that I know: Islam is engaged surrender, which is conscientiously acting and being in line with the greatest harmony of the universe, that which is the will of the Creator. It doesn't take a rocket scientist to note that any human being is capable of surrender. Nor does it take much to realize that while both of these definitions point to the self-evident, still patriarchy and disharmony with the creation reign unabashedly.

Muslim Women Participate Widely

I want to start with cosmology, with the way of the creation, but I think for this first entry I will skip the theology and instead go for the more politically expedient. In today's anthropology, Muslim women participate at every level of society and in every role, somewhere. In addition, in every Muslim context, minority or majority, in every class from the very poor or basic to the very wealthy and affluent, Muslim women are active in the promotion of their own well-being as well as the well-being of others. *Every*where.

Certainly the scope of their activities or the impact will vary according to many factors, but we need to put to rest the notion that we are waiting to be saved.

Especially when the idea of being saved is also linked with being saved *from* Islam. More Muslim women (and men for that matter) identify with being Muslim than any other religion in the world. Yep, even though we are only the second largest religion, we are the first with regard to identity. Muslims *like* being Muslim. And in case this is not self-evident, Muslim women *like* being Muslim women. It is sometimes scary for folks who can take or leave their own religious affiliations to understand just how important identity as a Muslim means to the vast majority of Muslims. But take it like you take the other aspects of identity: mothers identify as mothers, alcoholics identify (anonymously notwithstanding) as alcoholics, African Americans as African Americans, Muslims as Muslims. We identify with Islam. Even when pressed by bad publicity and bad actions by some of us, we still identify with Islam.

Either/Or Is the Prevailing Misconception

Why do people still think Muslim women must choose between identity as Muslims and identity with freedoms, human rights, dignity and democracy? For the first few decades of my work on gender I refused to accept the label "feminist," because of the politics of its use in the West. I gave my own title: pro-faith, pro-feminist. I was adamant that I would not bargain one against the other.

This is probably because in the context of the West, the first time we begin to hear about Muslim women, we hear about them from someone other than Muslim women. Muslim men or non-Muslim women were our chief spokespersons. When that shifted, a strange and depressing trend took over: Muslim women speaking for Islam and women who were disenfranchised with Islam.

So when [Ayaan] Hirsi Ali says she is a Muslim woman, we get to take for granted that her personal story is in fact reflective of most Muslim women's stories—and why do we need to think otherwise? She confirms what they like to hear in the West. You cannot have both Islam and human rights, so do away with Islam in favor of human rights. If it is either/or, then take rights.

Fortunately, by the skin of our teeth, Muslim women who not only identified with Islam but also took the challenge of improving their lives as Muslims and with the whole of the lived reality of Islam finally stopped just working so hard for that improvement and also began to self-represent. They were always there. But whether or not the international community knew about them, or about their work, was inconsequential. Or so they thought.

Both/And in Modern Islamic Feminism

So in the void, the story of the Muslim woman went from Muslim male and non-Muslim female spokespersons to anti-Islam Muslim spokeswomen. Finally we get to the women

Islamic Feminism Has a Long History

Long before the phrase "Islamic feminism" was coined, leading Muslim women intellectuals like the Moroccan writer and academic Fatema Mernissi, and Dr Asma Lamrabet, a Moroccan paediatrician, were writing and speaking for Muslim women's rights and equality, and for the re-reading of the Quran.

Victoria Brittain, "Islamic Feminists on the Move,"
Guardian, *January 29, 2007. www.guardian.co.uk.*

who straddled the divide between living Islam and living in the world today, so they challenge Islam to stay true to their realities. Then it was okay for me to let go of the cumbersome identification and have both Islam and human rights. There really never was a conflict in the first place; just a set of circumstances that caused the confusion that one had to choose between one and the other, instead of living both.

So, Islamic feminism was born. According to some, Islamic feminism always existed, but I defer to the concomitant set of circumstances that allowed for this self-naming to occur over that historical read. And this is my reasoning: At the earlier part of Islamic history there was no real radical understanding of gender. Yes there were gender roles, and there was patriarchy; lots of patriarchy. Everybody practiced patriarchy. It was not peculiar to Islam.

When we begin, as a human community, to examine gender as an aspect of knowledge, society and religion then we needed to go back and apply that category to everything we invested in as human beings. The feminist movement in the West, the second wave in particular, was very good at challenging gender inequities in every area—every discipline, except religion. Apparently religion was just too broken. So to choose "feminist," meant to do away with religion.

Muslim women, at the beginning of the 20th century, were engaged in nationalist movements, that included looking at gender and gender roles without critically examining the underlying anti-religion bias of much of the feminist movements. So they lived a divided life: Muslim in the private sphere but nationalist, democratic, socialist or whatever in the public sphere, supporting this religion/secular divide. It is possible to be Muslim and to be secular at the same time.

For me, a Muslim feminist is a secular Muslim and a secular feminist. Her methodologies do not include religious reform. She or he can choose from whatever means necessary to achieve the aims of empowerment. The better means for most secular Muslims would be the U.N. [United Nations] instruments like CEDAW (the Convention on the Elimination of [All Forms of] Discrimination Against Women). If there appears to be a conflict between the documents and Islam, then the documents should rule.

The Rise of the Islamists

Of course that did not sit well with the vast majority of Muslims who identify with Islam so the next voice that rose, we tend to call the fundamentalists, the neo-conservatives, whom finally we came to call (as they call themselves) the Islamists. Again the idea was, well, if there is a conflict between the international instruments and Islam, then, we take Islam. The either/or stand again.

Islamic feminism takes the responsibility to define Islam. It takes responsibility to critically examine the primary sources, the Qur'an, the *sunnah*, the *hadith*, and the *fiqh* or jurisprudence, and then to challenge both Islam and secular human rights standards. The basic underlying rule is justice, divine justice in fact. So the argument goes like this: Justice and equality are my divine right and anybody, any law, any interpretation that tries to take that away from me takes away my divine right and must be challenged. The basis of that challenge is in the divine sources themselves removed from the patriarchal context of their origins, developments and even current cultural background.

Islamic feminism takes responsibility for the formulation of Islam as a living reality. We are a part of that formation and we make the present and the future as we live it. Therefore there is no either/or. We are both Muslim and free. We are both in surrender and human beings. Anything that comes in between that, no matter how long it has been going on, and no matter how many people are in favor of it, is in fact a violation of the rights due to us from Allah. It is our duty to uphold that truth.

Islamic feminism is not just about equality in the public space but also in the family, where most gender roles are prescribed and gender inequality is fixed. Islamic feminism takes responsibility for our souls and our bodies, our minds and our contributions at every level. We take inspiration from our own relationships with the sacred and with the community to forge a way that enhances the quality of our lives and the lives of all others.

Personally, I want to thank the women and the men who see this as a mandate of our time: We will no longer live in the shadow of misrepresentation or under representation, we represent ourselves and we fight the good fight—the one that benefits everyone equally.

> *"The deception at the heart of the feminist movement is nowhere more apparent than in the silence with which self-professed feminists and feminist movements ignore the inhumane treatment of women who live under Islamic law."*

Western Feminism Ignores the Abuse of Women Under Islamic Law

Caroline B. Glick

Caroline B. Glick is deputy managing editor of the Jerusalem Post *and a senior fellow for Middle East affairs at the Center for Security Policy. In the following viewpoint, she contends that Western feminists and activists are overly concerned with Israel's occupation of the West Bank and not nearly engaged enough in combating sexism in Muslim countries. According to Glick, feminism in the West is deceptive in that it is in reality more interested in advancing a leftist agenda than in protecting the rights of women. Glick argues that Muslim crimes against women are common even in Western countries and that the silence of left-*

wing feminists and human rights organizations is partially responsible for the proliferation of such violence. Glick further maintains that by not fully supporting Israel the West provides Middle Eastern Muslim countries with no reason to advance women's rights.

As you read, consider the following questions:

1. According to Glick, what is the only country in the Middle East that defends human rights?

2. According to Glick, which advertisement did *Ms.* magazine refuse to run in 2008?

3. In which country was Sakineh Mohammadi Ashtiani found guilty of adultery and sentenced to death by stoning, according to Glick?

Making the rounds on YouTube these days is a film of a group of manly looking women preparing for and conducting a "flash dance" in a Philadelphia food store. The crew of ladies, dressed in tight black clothes and sequined accessories, arrives at the Fresh Grocer supermarket, breaks into a preplanned chant ordering shoppers not to buy Sabra and Tribe hummus and telling them to oppose Israeli "apartheid" and support "Palestine."

From their attire and attitude, it is fairly clear that the participants in the video would congratulate themselves on their commitment to the downtrodden, the wretched of the earth suffering under the jackboot of the powerful. They would likely all also describe themselves as feminists.

But if being a human rights activist means attacking the only country in the Middle East that defends human rights, then that means that at the very basic level, the term "human rights activist" is at best an empty term. And if being a feminist means attacking the only country in the Middle East where women enjoy freedom and equal rights, then feminism too, has become at best, a meaningless term. Indeed, if these anti-Israel female protesters are feminists then feminism is dead.

A Contradictory Defense of Women

In 1995, then First Lady Hillary Clinton spoke at the Fourth World Conference on Women in Beijing. There Clinton seemed to embrace the role of championing the rights of women and human rights worldwide when she proclaimed, "It is no longer acceptable to discuss women's rights as separate from human rights. . . . If there is one message that echoes forth from this conference, let it be that human rights are women's rights and women's rights are human rights, once and for all."

Yet as secretary of state, Hillary Clinton—like her fellow self-described feminists—has chosen to single Israel out for opprobrium while keeping nearly mum on the institutionalized, structural oppression of women and girls throughout the Muslim world. In so acting, Clinton is of course, loyally representing the views of the [President Barack] Obama administration she serves. She is also representing the views of the ideological left in which Clinton, US President Barack Obama, the human rights and feminist movements are all deeply rooted.

Since the height of the feminist movement in the late 1960s, non-leftist women in the West and Israel have been hard-pressed to answer the question of whether or not we are feminists. Non-leftist women are opposed to the oppression of women. Certainly, we are no less opposed to the oppression of women than leftist women are.

But at its most basic level, the feminist label has never been solely or even predominantly about preventing and ending oppression or discrimination of women. It has been about advancing the Left's social and political agenda against Western societies. It has been about castigating societies where women enjoy legal rights and protections as "structurally" discriminatory against women in order to weaken the legal, moral and social foundations of those societies. That is, rather than being about advancing the cause of women, to a large extent, the feminist movement has used the language of women's rights to advance a social and political agenda that has nothing to do with women.

So to a large degree, the feminist movement itself is a deception.

The deception at the heart of the feminist movement is nowhere more apparent than in the silence with which self-professed feminists and feminist movements ignore the inhumane treatment of women who live under Islamic law. If feminism weren't a hollow term, then prominent feminists should be the leaders of the anti-jihad movement.

Gloria Steinem and her sisters should be leading to call for the overthrow of the anti-female mullocracy in Iran and the end of gender apartheid in Saudi Arabia.

Instead, in 2008 *Ms.* magazine, which Steinem founded and which has served as the mouthpiece of the American feminist movement, refused to run an ad featuring then foreign minister Tzipi Livni, Supreme Court president Dorit Beinisch and then speaker of the Knesset Dalia Itzik that ran under the headline, "This is Israel."

It was too partisan, the magazine claimed.

Widespread Abuse

Leading feminist voices in the US and Europe remain unforgivably silent on the unspeakable oppression of women and girls in Islamic societies. And this cannot simply be attributed to a lack of interest in international affairs. Islamic subjugation and oppression of women happens in Western countries as well. Genital mutilation, forced marriage and other forms of abuse are widespread.

Western Feminists Have Ignored the Abuse of Muslim Women

It is frequently argued that honor killings, like female genital mutilation (FGM) have nothing to do with Islam. This does not explain why such abuses of women take place predominantly in Muslim societies. In today's climate of cultural relativism where Westerners do not wish to find fault with abuses of women under Islam, the voices of famous so-called feminists are either quiet, or even refuse to acknowledge that such abuse has anything to do with them. . . .

In Britain, and in an increasing number in North America, there are Muslim women who live in fear of their families. A friend of mine, who is now an apostate from Islam, was once thrown out of a moving car by her husband for not wearing her "hijab". She still fears her own family's reprisals. I personally have known Muslim women who live in dread of their families, because they have had relationships with Hindus or Sikhs.

Even though some women proudly proclaim themselves as feminists, where are the feminist voices to stand up for the rights of these women who live in fear?

With feminists like this, who needs enemies?

Adrian Morgan,
"The Failure of Western Feminists to Address Islamist Abuse,"
Family Security Matters, *December 17, 2007.*
www.familysecuritymatters.org.

For instance, every year hundreds of Muslim women and girls in Western countries are brutally murdered by their male relatives in so-called "honor killings."

Pamela Geller, the intrepid blogger at *Atlas Shrugs*, has steadfastly documented every case she has found. This year [2010] she ran an ad campaign on public buses and taxis in major US cities to bring public awareness to their plight. And for her singular efforts in championing the right to life of Muslim women and girls, she has been reviled by the Left as an anti-Islamic bigot.

Former Dutch parliamentarian Ayaan Hirsi Ali was forced to flee Holland and live surrounded by bodyguards for the past six years because she has made an issue of Islamic oppression of women and girls. The Left—including the feminist movement—has treated this remarkable former Muslim and champion of women's rights as a leper.

If all the feminist community's policy of ignoring Islamic oppression of women did was keep it out of the headlines it would still be unforgivable. But the fact is that by not speaking of the central challenge to women's rights in our times, the organized feminist movement, and the Left it is a part of, are abetting Islam's unspeakable crimes against women and girls. It does so in two ways.

Tyranny unchallenged is tyranny abetted.

An International Outcry

And the first way that the organized feminist movement and the Left abet the oppression of women by Islamic authorities is signaling to those authorities that they can get away with it. This truth is laid bare by the responses of Islamic authorities in the rare cases where their oppression of women has received Western attention.

For instance, in 2006, an Iranian Islamic court found Sakineh Mohammadi Ashtiani guilty of adultery and sentenced the ethnic Azeri kindergarten teacher and mother of two to death by stoning. She was later also found guilty of murdering her husband.

Ashtiani's confessions in both cases were extracted under torture. She has already received 99 lashes for her reputed initial crime. Not a Farsi or Arabic speaker, when her adultery trial ended, Ashtiani didn't even know she was convicted or what her sentence was.

In recent years, Ashtiani's children assisted by Iranian émigré and non-leftist human rights groups launched a courageous campaign to save her life. Over the past year, the campaign was covered in the Western media and garnered the support of notables such as the French and Canadian prime ministers' wives as well as international film stars like Lindsay Lohan, Colin Firth, Emma Thompson, Robert Redford and Juliette Binoche.

Human Rights Watch and Amnesty International got on board this past summer and decried her treatment. Clinton herself gave a half sentence condemnation of Ashtiani's persecution in August. Indeed, the international attention focused on Ashtiani may have been the reason the Obama administration belatedly voiced opposition to Iran's election to the new UN [United Nations] women's rights council. Iran was elected by acclamation in April, but later defeated by India when a roll call vote was called.

Reeling from this criticism, Iranian authorities began backtracking. First they claimed Ashtiani's death sentence would be cancelled.

Then they said she would be hanged rather than stoned. Today her fate remains unclear and her life is still in grave danger.

But if pressure on Iranian authorities keeps up, there is a reasonable chance that Ashtiani's long ordeal will end in life, rather than death.

Ashtiani's case is proof that when the West makes the barbaric abuse of women an issue, the Islamic world attenuates its abuse of women. Pressure works. In contrast, an absence of pressure empowers the oppressors.

Leftist Attacks on Israel

The second way that the feminists and the Left they are a part of abet Islamic oppression of women is through their animosity towards Israel. When the Shariah-besotted leaders of the Muslim world see the Western left devote its energies to attacking Israel—the only human rights and women's rights protecting country in the Middle East—they see there is no reason for them to reconsider their willingness to tyrannize their women and girls.

Take Indonesia for example. In 2003, then Indonesian president Megawati Sukarnoputri agreed that as part of a cease-fire agreement, the separatist Aceh province was allowed to institute Shariah law as the law of the province. In 2009, the Aceh parliament passed a law making adultery punishable by stoning. On the central squares of the province that is home to four million, people are routinely publicly whipped for offenses against Islam.

Just last Friday, Anis Saputra, 24, and Kiki Hanafilia, 17, each received eight lashes in a public ceremony outside a local mosque for being caught kissing in October. The two are reportedly married to other people and they apparently were given lashes rather than stoned to death because they had yet to consummate their alleged romance.

Last year the province also forbade women and girls from wearing pants. A France 24 investigation of Shariah in Aceh showed a traumatized 14-year-old girl who was beset by Islamic police on her way home from school. They cut her jeans off in the middle of the street.

Yet rather than criticize Indonesia for these appalling developments, last month Obama visited Jakarta and waxed poetic about Islamic tolerance of differences and applauded Indonesia for its commitment to democracy.

And while ignoring Indonesia's repressive Shariah-ruled province where Islamic oppression is the rule not the exception, Obama devoted his criticism to attacking Israel for allowing Jews to build homes in Jerusalem.

There is no doubt that attitudes that discriminate against women exist today in Western countries as well as in Israel.

Women in the free world have unique challenges to overcome because of our gender.

But a sense of proportion is required here.

These challenges are not overwhelming, systemic or in most cases life threatening.

On the other hand, hundreds of millions of women and girls throughout the Islamic world are terrorized daily by everyone from their families to their judges. They have no reason to believe that if challenged their rights—even their right to life—will be protected.

The fact that the ladies in Philadelphia decided to take their stand against Israel and that Clinton and Obama attack Israel for building homes for Jews in Jerusalem, Judea and Samaria while they all ignore the suffering of the women of Islam speaks volumes about the degradation of the West under the Left's social and political leadership.

It also tells non-leftist women in the West that being pro-women's rights and being a feminist are increasingly mutually exclusive.

> "While the patriarchal view, which holds that women are subordinate in their role and their very being, has been around for much of history, it was only in the 1970s that a new patriarchal religious strain emerged within the evangelical community."

Traditional Evangelical Christian Doctrine Advocates Gender Equality and Social Justice

Mimi Haddad

Mimi Haddad is president of Christians for Biblical Equality and a founding member of the Evangelicals and Gender Steering Committee at the Evangelical Theological Society. She has published widely on issues related to gender and Christianity. In the following viewpoint, she explores the historical role of women in evangelical Christianity, noting that women and former slaves traditionally held leadership roles in the movement, including working in the ministry as preachers. Explaining that it was only with the rise of a form of patriarchalism in the evangelical

Mimi Haddad, "Empowered by God: The Rich History of Evangelical Feminism," *Sojourners*, August 2009. Copyright © 2009 by Sojourners Magazine. Reprinted with permission from Sojourners. 1-800-714-7474, www.sojo.net.

church called "complementarianism" in the 1970s, that the belief that men and women were created to fulfill different roles and functions in both the church and in the family became popularized. According to Haddad, the written works of the Christian apostles, particularly St. Paul, represented a radical reinterpretation of human life, offering equality to women, slaves, and all nationalities before being overtaken by the patriarchal church in the early centuries of Christianity. Protestant denominations of the 1800s, on the other hand, allowed for great freedom for women in the ministry and encouraged social justice activism.

As you read, consider the following questions:

1. According to Haddad, what act of faith did early evangelicals believe to be the most significant in a person's life?

2. Which women in Protestant history worked alongside men in advancing the faith, according to the viewpoint?

3. What term does Haddad use to describe Katharine Bushnell and others who believed in the principle of Christian equality during the 1800s?

One of my friends works in Christian ministry at a large, secular university. She is passionate about Christ; she is a gifted teacher, preacher, and apologist; she has dedicated her life to loving college students. She is tenacious in using her spiritual gifts and willing to live on a very limited salary. And, as she told me, "My church spends thousands of dollars so I can share the gospel with college students, both men and women. Yet they will not permit me to preach from the pulpit because I am a woman. This is not only inconsistent. What is worse, they are telling me that there is something wrong with being female!"

However, in the memory of those still living, things have been very different in the evangelical movement. Recently, three women in their 80s came into the office of Christians for Biblical Equality to volunteer. All three attended evangelical churches. All three were raised evangelical and went to Wheaton College. And all three remember hearing of female evangelists such as Amy Lee Stockton and Rita Gould preaching throughout the Midwest, in places that would surprise some of us today. One of the women, Alvera Mickelsen, told me, "You know, it wasn't until 1950 that women preachers were considered 'liberal.' Before that, no one thought twice about women preaching the gospel."

The Rise of the Complementarians

The contrast between the experience of these women and that of many evangelicals in college today tells us that something vital has been lost for evangelicals. While the patriarchal view, which holds that women are subordinate in their role and their very being, has been around for much of history, it was only in the 1970s that a new patriarchal religious strain emerged within the evangelical community: the so-called "complementarian" view, which argues that, while men and women are created in God's image as equals, women have different "roles" or "functions" than men. By "role" or "function" they mean one thing: that women are to be submissive to male authority.

This dissonance between what women are (created equally by God) and what they are to do (take a subordinate role to men) is a challenge to logic. But is it also a challenge to Christian history and scripture? In fact, what evangelical "complementarians" are missing is the fact that the shared authority and ministry of men and women were embraced in egalitarian ways in the work of the apostles—and in the writings and ministry of the early evangelicals of the 1700s.

Because early evangelicals believed that conversion marks the clearest division in life, they included all believers in the work of evangelism, even if it meant challenging social taboos by giving women and slaves new positions of leadership and

Christianity and Feminism Share Some Common Ground

The history of Western feminism reminds us that our concepts of liberation and equality are not always antithetical to the Christian tradition and that Christian theology and Scripture have served as a source of women's liberation.

Regan Penaluna,
"Christianity and Feminism: Oil and Water?"
First Things, *March 26, 2009. www.firstthings.com.*

freedom. The priority they gave to evangelism loosened the grip of prejudice within the body of Christ, challenging the patriarchal assumptions that dominated church culture after the death of the apostles.

To appreciate the roots of this break that evangelicals made with patriarchy, let us consider how the earliest Christian church—that of New Testament times—had made its own break from the society in which it arose. Remember, the Christian church emerged in a society where most gender expectations had been shaped by Greek philosophy, which assumed that women's ontology—their being, nature, or essence—was less morally pure, rational, or strong compared to men's. As Aristotle put it in the fourth century B.C.E., "the relationship between the male and the female is by nature such that . . . the male rules and the female is ruled." And such philosophical assumptions had consequences in everyday life: Women in the ancient world had no authority in decision making within social structures, and vast numbers of girl babies were exposed—left in the open to die—after birth.

Women in the New Testament

Consider how differently the church in New Testament times functioned! Women—Priscilla, Junia, Lydia, Chloe, Nympha, Apphia, Phoebe, and more—served in positions of leadership. Baptism, open to both men and women, replaced circumcision as the outer expression of our inner relationship with Christ. Women were not required to be obedient, but to offer voluntary submission, just as Paul asks all Christians to submit to one another (Ephesians 5:21).

When Paul wrote in Galatians 3:28 that Jews and Greeks, slaves and free, male and female, are all one in Christ, he offered these words to a culture in which nearly half of all people were slaves and more than half were female. His words are radical indeed when you consider that, in Paul's culture, your identity and sphere of influence were determined by your gender, ethnicity, and class. To this world Paul boldly declares that our value and influence come not from our parents but from God, from whom we receive our ultimate inheritance, and our sisters and brothers in Christ receive the same inheritance equally from God's Spirit. Rebirth in Christ opens opportunities for equality of function within Christ's new covenant community.

Sadly, after the death of the apostles, the church adopted the cultural devaluation of women. As [Saint John] Chrysostom (347–407 C.E.) put it, "The woman taught once, and ruined all. On this account therefore he saith, let her not teach ... for the sex is weak and fickle." Throughout the Middle Ages, while women such as Catherine of Siena, Hildegard, and Theodora provided moral leadership to the church during war, conflict, corruption, and the plague, theologians such as [Thomas] Aquinas continued to argue that women were inferior in nature and service. Later, Protestant reformers such as John Calvin and John Knox kept rank with the patriarchal assumptions of earlier theologians, even though women were prominent in advancing Protestant faith throughout Europe.

Women such as Lady Jane Grey in England; Jeanne D'Albret—defender of the Huguenots—in France; and Katharina von Bora, Martin Luther's wife, in Germany courageously promoted Protestant faith, even though many were tortured and martyred.

The egalitarian view of the New Testament church began to re-emerge in 1666 with the writings of the Quaker Margaret Fell Fox. It gained enormous momentum in the 1800s, during what has been called the "golden era" of missions—the largest missionary impulse the world has ever known. New centers of Christian strength and vitality were flourishing in the Americas, Africa, and Asia, according to mission experts such as Dana Robert. More than half of all Christians were found outside the region that had been the historical heartland of Christianity for nearly 1,500 years. In all of this, women, who outnumbered men on mission fields 2-to-1, played a central role; so did people, such as Amanda Smith who had been born into slavery.

Missions Redefine Women's Role

The success of women and former slaves as missionaries called into question gender and ethnic bias in interpreting scripture—and the church began to see the importance of liberating them both in church and in society. Between 1808 and 1930, more than 46 biblical publications were issued in support of women's gospel leadership. These documents signify the emergence of the first wave of feminists—a movement that was deeply biblical.

For example, A.J. Gordon (1836–95), perhaps the most prominent evangelical pastor of his day, was a leading advocate of abolition, missions, and women in ministry. Gordon believed that Pentecost was the "Magna Carta of the Christian church," in which those who had once been viewed as inferior by natural birth (their being and nature) attain a new spiritual status through the power of the Holy Spirit. God's gifting no longer rests on a "favored few, but upon the many, without regard to race, or age, or sex."

Perhaps the most extensive egalitarian reading of the Bible was advanced by Dr. Katharine Bushnell (1856–1946), a medical doctor, missionary, Bible translator, and activist who exemplified the period's combination of missionary work, social activism, and first wave feminism. Her book *God's Word to Women*, released in 1919 and still in print, advanced the equality of women—a position that grew out of her study of scripture in the original languages, her observations of women's leadership on the mission field, and her medical efforts to help abused women both in the U.S. and in India.

Bushnell begins her theological basis for women's equality in Genesis, by observing that Adam and Eve were both equally created in God's image and called to share dominion in Eden. Satan, not Eve, was the source of sin (Genesis 3:14–15), and sin led to the domination of men over women (Genesis 3:16). Most important, Bushnell and other evangelical egalitarians assessed women's essence and capacity for ministry—just like men's—based not on the Fall, but on Christ's victory at Calvary.

The egalitarians of the 1800s affirmed the authority of the scriptures and provided a challenge to the presumed inferiority of women and slaves, as it had been put forward by previous generations of Christians. Ultimately, first wave feminists offered a serious blow to any biblical support for determining one's scope of service based on attributes such as gender, class, or ethnicity.

Early feminists not only established the hermeneutical groundwork for later generations of egalitarians to build upon; they also fueled activism that dealt a deathblow to the institution of slavery and made it possible for women to gain the right to vote and become preachers of the gospel. As we can see, the liberation of women was a deeply biblical movement;

it began not with secular feminists such as Gloria Steinem in the 1970s, as is often argued, but with Katharine Bushnell, Amanda Smith, and A.J. Gordon in the 1800s and earlier.

The priority given to conversion, so highly valued by evangelicals, pressed them to give women and slaves new ministry opportunities. The call of evangelism can press us today to acknowledge and embrace the gospel leadership of women—empowered by God since the empty tomb!

"The core ideology was a direct contradiction of Roe v. Wade: *Women's bodies and lives did not belong to them, but to God and his plans for Christian revival."*

Fundamentalist Christian Patriarchy Endangers Women and Children

Kathryn Joyce

Kathryn Joyce is a New York–based journalist and the author of Quiverfull: Inside the Christian Patriarchy Movement. *In the following viewpoint, she talks to Vyckie Garrison, a mother of seven who left the Quiverfull community after her oldest daughter tried to commit suicide from the stress of the group's strict tenets of female submission and prolific childbearing. Joyce explains that some of Quiverfull's core principles maintain that contraception leads to abortion and that feminism is un-Christian. Joyce and Garrison discuss Garrison's gradual realization that her life of constant pregnancy, housework, and homeschooling—a fundamental element of the Quiverfull movement—could not be sustained without damage to herself or her children,*

Kathryn Joyce, "All God's Children," Salon.com, March 14, 2009, Copyright © 2010 by Salon.com. This article first appeared in Salon.com, at http://www.salon.com. An online version remains in the Salon archives. Reprinted with permission.

despite being named family of the year by the Nebraska Family Council in 2003. According to Joyce, the Quiverfull movement is growing in numbers and influence, and women who leave the group often are shunned.

As you read, consider the following questions:

1. According to Joyce, how many children do Quiverfull women have on average?

2. When did the Quiverfull movement begin, according to Joyce?

3. In addition to multiple unplanned pregnancies, what kind of birth does Quiverfull encourage, according to the viewpoint?

Vyckie Garrison wasn't sure she wanted to use her real name in this article. Until last year [2008], Garrison (then Vyckie Bennett), a 43-year-old single mother of seven living in Norfolk, Neb., followed a fundamentalist pronatalist theology known as Quiverfull. Shunning all forms of birth control, Quiverfull women accept as many children as God gives them as a demonstration of their radical faith and obedience, as well as a means to advance his kingdom: winning the country for Christ by having more children than their adversaries. This self-proclaimed "patriarchy" movement, which likely numbers in the tens of thousands but which is growing exponentially, bases its arguments on Psalm 127: "Like arrows in the hands of a warrior are sons born in one's youth. Blessed is the man whose quiver is full of them. They shall not be put to shame when they contend with their enemies in the gate." Quiverfull women commonly give birth to families of eight, 10 and 12 children, or more.

Unlike TV's *Big Love* polygamists or traditionally large Catholic and Mormon families, the Quiverfull conviction does not follow from any official church doctrine. It's a cross-denominational movement among evangelical and fundamentalist Protestants who have adopted some Catholic arguments against contraception and who have spread their ideas through the booming conservative homeschooling community.

Quiverfull has gained exposure through cable TV's fascination with extraordinarily large families, including the 18-child Duggar family. The Duggars, an Arkansas couple whose husband Jim Bob was a former Arkansas state representative, have appeared on several Discovery Health Channel specials about their immense brood and currently have a TLC reality show, *18 Kids and Counting* [currently known in 2012 as *19 Kids and Counting*], that focuses on the saccharine details of large family life.

Women Belong to God

But there's a lot more to the Quiverfull conviction than you see on the Duggars' folksy show. In 1985, homeschooling leader Mary Pride wrote a foundational text for Quiverfull, *The Way Home: Beyond Feminism, Back to Reality*. The book argued that family planning is a slippery slope, creating a "contraceptive mentality" that leads to abortion, and that feminism is incompatible with Christianity. As an antidote, Pride told Christians to reject women's liberation in exchange for the principles of submissive wifehood and prolific stay-at-home motherhood. The core ideology was a direct contradiction of *Roe v. Wade*: Women's bodies and lives did not belong to them, but to God and his plans for Christian revival.

Since 1985, Quiverfull has been thriving in the southern and Sunbelt states. Although the conviction of "letting God plan your family" is not an official doctrine in many churches, there are signs of its acceptance in high places; the Rev. Albert Mohler, Theological Seminary president of the 16-million-member Southern Baptist Convention, argued, for example, that deliberate childlessness was "moral rebellion" against God.

While researching my book, *Quiverfull: Inside the Christian Patriarchy Movement*, over the past several years, I spoke with dozens of women who follow the Quiverfull conviction. I also met a handful who had left the movement and now denounce the lifestyle as one of unceasing labor and exhaustion—a near-constant cycle of pregnancy, childbirth and the care of small children—for the women at its center.

Vyckie Garrison is one of those who lost faith in the movement. For years, she was among its lay leadership. She homeschooled her seven children, from her 23-year-old daughter, Angel, to her 6-year-old son, Wesley, and was active in Quiverfull's popular sterilization reversal ministries. She ran a monthly conservative family newspaper that published some of the movement's foremost advocates. The Bennetts were even named Nebraska's "family of the year" in 2003 by the Nebraska Family Council.

"You couldn't have found a more godly family," says Garrison, a sharp-witted and frank woman who has updated her look since leaving the movement—cutting her nearly waist-length blond hair and wearing light makeup to highlight an engaging smile.

Difficulties Below the Surface

She may have looked like the perfect Quiverfull wife, but Garrison was struggling to care for her seven children, three of whom have a rare bone disease, while juggling the demands of her husband and coping with difficult pregnancies. Though she preached patriarchy to her readers, practicing it at home required a major suspension of disbelief. Her husband, Warren, had been blinded in a work accident years earlier and had trouble keeping a job. Garrison founded her paper in part to create a sales position for him, to maintain the illusion of his heading their family. But Warren chafed against his dependency and was verbally abusive, Garrison says, browbeating her and the children into frightened compliance.

Garrison hadn't come to Quiverfull from a fundamentalist background. She grew up in an unstable household, moving frequently around Nevada with her mother and her mother's series of live-in boyfriends who molested her sister; she was rarely in school long enough to fulfill the potential her high grades indicated. At 16, she married a high school boyfriend in a friend's disheveled apartment and walked home in her wedding dress from a honeymoon in a nearby motel. They moved to Carson City, subsisting on Job Corps positions and crashing with hard-partying friends. In despair, Garrison found God while listening to a Christian radio station one night. When she began attending a Pentecostal church, a group of older, middle-class women shepherded the teenage Garrison through the basic lessons of biblical womanhood and submission, starting with the admonition that for wives, love is not a feeling but a choice. Garrison looked to her mentors as beacons of propriety, "like Princess Diana," she says, giving her a glimpse of a better world.

Garrison's marriage ended, and she became pregnant with her oldest daughter, Angel, during a short-lived rebound affair. She moved to Iowa to be near her mother and met Warren at a church picnic. After getting married, Garrison followed a new pastor's counsel to homeschool her growing family, which eventually led her to the Quiverfull movement, where homeschooling, Quiverfull and submission are intertwined convictions. As Garrison says, "If you take one, you pretty much have to take it all eventually."

Accepting every pregnancy as a unilateral blessing meant some radical leaps of faith, however. Put into physical practice, Garrison says the lesson of leaders like Nancy Campbell, editor of the fundamentalist women's magazine *Above Rubies* and author of movement books like *Be Fruitful and Multiply*, "was, if pregnancy can kill you, think of the missionaries who go off to foreign lands and put their lives on the line. It's no

On the Life of Quiverfull Daughters

A Quiverfull daughter is taught from a young age that her purpose in life is to serve the man whom God has placed in authority over her. She serves her father while she lives at home (she does this primarily by assisting her mother in domestic duties and child care). She absolutely must remain a virgin and is taught to expect to meet and marry her future husband through a father-led match-making process called "courtship." Her education is geared toward developing domestic skills—college is generally considered unnecessary and even dangerous for her spiritual well-being.

Sarah Jones, "Born to Breed:
An Interview with Quiverfull Walkaway Vyckie Garrison,"
PoliticusUSA, June 25, 2011. www.politicususa.com

different if you're risking your own body or life." Indeed, Mary Pride referred to her mothers as "maternal missionaries."

A Life of Sacrifice

Garrison complied. She'd had her first three children by cesarean section, but after coming to the Quiverfull conviction, she was swayed by the movement's emphasis on natural (even unassisted home) birth. During one delivery, she suffered a partial uterine rupture and "felt like I'd been in a major battle with Satan, and he'd just about left me dead." The doctor who treated Garrison lectured her for an hour not to conceive again, but she felt that stopping on her own would be rebellion. When she turned to her leaders for inspiration, she received a bleak message: that if she died doing her maternal duty, God would care for her family. For six months, she couldn't look at the baby without crying.

For much of that time, her oldest daughter, Angel, effectively mothered the newborn—not at all uncommon in the Quiverfull community, where daughters learn early to follow their mothers in domestic service and sacrifice.

The strain began to weigh on Angel as well, though, and Garrison says her daughter began acting out: feigning injuries, bruising her own face and exaggerating stories of trouble at home when Garrison sent her to intern for Nancy Campbell—embellishments Garrison imagines sprang from Angel's inability to adequately convey her unhappiness to the fundamentalist believers around her. "She knew that something wasn't right, but she couldn't articulate it because we were family of the year."

Desperate, Angel made a clumsy suicide attempt with high doses of Tylenol and Maalox at the age of 21, checking herself into the emergency room after the attempt failed.

The episode shook Garrison, who drove from Norfolk to Nashville to retrieve Angel from a psychiatric ward. She began to see her younger children as joyless and traumatized. Trying to step between the children and Warren, she enraged him with her assertiveness. Her fatigue became overwhelming, and her blood pressure sank.

Garrison began corresponding with an intellectual atheist uncle whose gentle questions helped her acknowledge her mounting crisis of faith. She wrote her uncle: "If, as I kind of suspect, it turns out that I don't actually believe in a personal God, I know I'm going to be exceedingly pissed—knowing that I've done my best with the hand I've been dealt and it's cost me a lot and it's worn me down—only to discover midway through that the game is rigged and there's no way I can win."

Garrison fled to a friend in Kansas City for several weeks, though she eventually returned for her children, ending up in an ugly custody battle that she finally won.

When she told an editor at her paper that she was getting divorced, his first words were "Cheryl Lindsey"—a reference to Cheryl Lindsey Seelhoff, an early Quiverfull leader who left her husband and the movement and was subsequently denounced and run out of business by her homeschooling peers. "I think he was warning me," Garrison says.

Leaving the Community

The experience of Garrison's friend Laura—a mother of 11 who collapsed under the demands of the lifestyle—also helps explain why many unhappy women are afraid to turn their backs on the movement, when they'll be left with scant financial resources, years without work experience, and a dearth of references from a community that often shuns them. Laura was near suicide when Garrison helped her leave; her husband took physical custody of all 11 children, and her oldest daughter seamlessly assumed Laura's duties and tended to the younger children, who now view their mother as a backslider deceived by Satan. "She feels so incredibly angry, so ripped off, so used. Her new motto is 'F--- God.'"

"Me and Laura both say we hope we don't end up as atheists," says Garrison, with a laugh, though she can't think of herself as anything else. This month [March 2009], Laura and Garrison began a blog, cheekily named *No Longer Quivering* to describe their experiences exiting the movement. Currently, Garrison is attending a relatively liberal Salvation Army church in Norfolk. She doesn't go for the faith anymore, but for the people, people in "bad shape" who remind Garrison of her childhood friends. She affectionately jokes with the pastor's wife that she's glad they "don't take the Bible seriously."

For Garrison, taking the Bible seriously is synonymous with the punishing claims of the Quiverfull movement. But having lost her faith in the Bible-proofed patriarchy principles she was taught, Garrison is unable to accept any of it anymore. "I don't think you can get equality out of the Bible. You can't get away from hierarchy, strictly defined roles for gender, authoritarianism, submission, dominating." Many believers might take issue with that, but to devout believers of Quiverfull, patriarchy is simply "the logical conclusion of what Scripture teaches," Garrison says.

As for herself, Garrison says, "I gave my life to Jesus, and he didn't do with it what I would have done." She feels as though she's in free fall, her "feet planted firmly in midair," as the evangelical luminary Francis Schaeffer once remarked of non-Christians.

Sometimes it's exhilarating, but often she wonders when she'll hit the ground. The chaos and confusion that follow leaving the movement is a powerful deterrent to other women who face losing their children as Laura did, or becoming overwhelmed like Garrison. "The only thing that keeps these mothers going is they have incredible motivation," says Garrison. "They believe they're building the kingdom of God." Though her children are thriving in public school, Garrison struggles to find the energy to mother seven children without the incentive, and threat, that the Quiverfull conviction provides: a promise that obedient Christian wives may, through their meekness, their submission and their posterity, inherit the earth.

> "The historical association of black femininity with amorality, promiscuity and fallen womanhood makes the stakes for and investment in black female religiosity higher."

Christian Dogma Obstructs the Self-Determination of African American Women

Sikivu Hutchinson

Sikivu Hutchinson is a senior fellow at the Institute for Humanist Studies and the editor of BlackFemLens.org. In the following viewpoint, she argues that the white movement to Christianize female African slaves and their descendants was an effort to control their bodies and identities, casting them in a role of permanent servitude and personal sacrifice, because they were seen as savage and dangerously sexualized. The American black Christian church that arose, says Hutchinson, reinforced the patriarchal model of religion, and it was against this model that Sojourner Truth fought in the mid-nineteenth century. Hutchinson maintains that even the modern black church in the United States reinforces this racist and sexist gender identity through its

Sikivu Hutchinson, "Beyond the Sacrificial Good Woman: Freethinking and Black Feminism," *Hollywood Progressive*, October 29, 2010. Copyright © 2010 by Sikivu Hutchinson. All rights reserved. Reproduced by permission.

elaborate rites and rituals, as well as its internal power struc-
ture. In contrast, Hutchinson argues that black American women
such as Nella Larsen and Zora Neale Hurston rejected the white
Christian identity that had been forced upon them and instead
took up an ideology of secular humanism, becoming freethinkers.

As you read, consider the following questions:

1. What film does Hutchinson cite as an example of depic-
   tions of African American Christians?

2. According to Hutchinson, who was the "Hottentot Venus"?

3. What is the title of Sojourner Truth's most famous
   speech, according to the viewpoint?

In the 1997 film *The Apostle* Robert Duvall plays a white
Southern Christian fundamentalist preacher and murderer
on the lam seeking redemption. The film is literally cluttered
with images of devout blacks, from black women swaying in
the breeze at a big tent church revival to a particularly indel-
ible church scene of dozens of black men chanting "Jesus" in
rapturous response to Duvall's pulpit-pounding call.

I found *The Apostle* perversely fascinating because it trot-
ted out this totally revisionist romanticized narrative of black
obeisance to yet another charismatic but flawed white renegade savior figure in Louisiana (where, contrary to Hollywood flimflammery, most of the congregations are racially
segregated). These popular fantasies of black religiosity always
seem to revolve around images of good, matronly black
women eternally quivering with a strategic "Amen" or "can I
get a witness"; subject to break out into a Blues Brothers
backflip down the church aisle at any moment.

It's a caricature of black feminine servility—in homage to
the Lord, the good book and the white renegade—that exem-
plifies what Toni Morrison has characterized as the "service-

ability" of blackness and the black body. In her 1992 book, *Playing in the Dark: Whiteness and the Literary Imagination*, Morrison argues that blackness and the black body—or what she dubs the Africanist presence—have historically functioned as vehicles or props for white subjectivity. In 18th-century America, the Africanist presence allowed the new white man of the emergent slave republic to pose and explore fundamental questions about what it meant to be free, what it meant to [be] human and what it meant to be a citizen within a founding "democratic" society.

In 19th-century Europe, the Africanist presence was literally articulated through the exhibition of black bodies, most notably that of Saartjie Baartman, aka the so-called Hottentot Venus, a young South African Khoi woman. Baartman was paraded all over Europe and displayed in salons in museums by the European scientific establishment. For the hoards of gawking white spectators who paid to see her "perform," her "grotesquely exaggerated" anatomy demonstrated that there were clear boundaries between the civilized self and the savage sexually deviant Other.

When Black Women Construct Their Identities

Caught in the crossfire of science and superstition, black femininity has been critical to defining Western notions of "the human." Negotiating the journey to the human on their own terms has been a centuries' long quest for black women freethinkers, veering between religion and skepticism, faith and humanism. Bringing a black feminist secular humanist freethinking tradition "out of the closet" requires an assessment of the way black women have intervened in their historical construction as racial and sexual Others.

For example, when preacher and abolitionist Sojourner Truth purportedly rolled up her shirt sleeve during her historic 1851 "Ain't I a Woman?" speech before the Women's

Convention in Akron, Ohio, to show how many rows of cotton she'd plowed, she simultaneously rebuked notions of genteel white womanhood and degraded black femininity. By celebrating her flesh as a field slave and mother of several children "who didn't need to be helped over ditches," she was challenging the gendered division between body and intellect, men's space and women's space.

Black feminist secular humanism emerges from the legacy of Truth's humanist intervention into the dualities of Western empiricism and Judeo Christian dogma. Enlightenment and Judeo Christian ideologies of black racial otherness and black sexuality reinforced each other. Blackness was outside of the human, the rational, the sovereign, and, of course, the moral. While white women have traditionally been placed on pedestals, and idealized as the ultimate symbols of feminine virtue, worth and desirability, black women have been demonized as hypersexual Jezebels or asexual Aunt Jemimas. The historical association of black femininity with amorality, promiscuity and fallen womanhood makes the stakes for and investment in black female religiosity higher. Christianity was a means of redeeming "fallen" black femininity.

Truth, of course, was also challenging the authority of white male preachers who muscled in on the Akron convention to remind the sinful women activists that females who spoke in public were guilty of heresy. In her rebuttal she proclaimed: "Then that little man in black there, he says women can't have as much rights as men, 'cause Christ wasn't a woman! Where did your Christ come from? Where did your Christ come from? From God and a woman! Man had nothing to do with Him." Tweaking biblical literalism with her own feminist spin, Truth bequeathed us the paradoxical figure of the defiant black woman of faith, ever-ready with a bit of scripture (à la the take no prisoners Lena Wilder from Lorraine Hansbury's *A Raisin in the Sun*) to verbally smack down Christian fundamentalists and heathens-in-the-making alike.

Truth's example influenced a long line of activist women of faith, from the radical journalist/newspaper owners Ida B. Wells and Charlotta Bass, to civil rights firebrand Fannie Lou Hamer. Wells and Bass drew on humanist freethinking principles in their exhaustive exposes of lynching, racial terrorism and residential segregation. Hamer, an astute critic of the contradictions of Jim Crow "democracy," was beaten and jailed like a dog for fighting for the right to vote. Yet, in the post–civil rights era, these hybrid models of faith-based and humanist social justice activism have been largely eclipsed by that of the good woman of faith as backbone of an increasingly socially conservative, insular black church. Steadfastly devout, black women power all the numerous Pew Research [Center] studies which indicate that African Americans are one of the most religious groups in the country.

Black Christian Conformity

Black adoption of Christian dogma brought African Americans into conformity with European American sexist/heterosexist models of gender hierarchy. As historian Paula Giddings notes, the black church played a key role in enforcing black patriarchy because it "attempted to do this in much the same way that Whites had used religion, by putting a new emphasis on the biblical 'sanction for male ascendancy.'" This "new emphasis" meant that black men could be rightful patriarchs despite the yoke of slavery and Jim Crow apartheid. Contrary to the popular belief that black men were "emasculated" under slavery because they did not have unfettered access to and "control" over the bodies and destinies of black women and children, women were still socialized to fulfill gender hierarchical responsibilities like cooking, cleaning and taking care of children. Black women were still regarded as the primary caregivers of the family, the protectors of home, hearth and the well-being of their male partners and their children. Black women were the repositories of moral and social values, entrusted with transmitting them to children.

So because women are responsible for transmitting moral values to children and families, breaking from deeply ingrained Christian ideology, culture and community ties is problematic. In African American communities where devoutness is the "default position," the presumption of female religiosity, reinforced by cultural representation, is a binding influence that makes public skepticism for women taboo.

For observant women, questioning much less rejecting, religion would be just as counterintuitive as rejecting their connection to their lived experiences. In this regard religious observance is as much a performance and reproduction of gender identity as it is an exercise of personal "morality." Many of the rituals of black churchgoing forge this sense of gendered identity as community. From the often elaborate pageantry of dressing for church, to participation in church leadership bodies, to the process of instilling children with "proper" "Christian" values in church-affiliated day care centers and schools—the gendered social contract of organized religion is compulsorily drilled into many black women.

Self-Sacrifice and Skepticism

Perhaps no modern black woman writer and skeptic captured this more vividly than Nella Larsen. In her 1928 novel *Quicksand*, Larsen chronicles the claustrophobia of domesticity, religiosity and female self-sacrifice in African American community. After a long personal journey from skepticism to religious acquiescence, Larsen's mixed race protagonist Helga, a pastor's wife, eventually rejects the existence of God. Helga's internal conflict over the dominance of religious belief in the black community reaches a fever pitch after a long painful convalescence from childbirth. Throughout the novel Helga frequently disdains blacks' passive acceptance of "the White man's God." For Helga "Religion after all, had its uses. It blunted the per-

Beverly Guy-Sheftall on Black Feminism

Now ... black feminist thought is very much an important part of a broader women's studies—it would be very difficult to avoid black feminism when speaking about a more general feminism. What's interesting, though, is that black feminism is still very much a suspect politic in black spaces. Despite our progress, it seems that in some hetero-patriarchal paradigms, like black studies and black culture, feminism seems to be less accepted.

Akoto Ofori Atta,
"The Root Interview: Beverly Guy-Sheftall on Black Feminism,"
The Root, *November 24, 2010. www.theroot.com.*

ceptions. Robbed life of its crudest truths. Especially it had uses for the poor—for the blacks." Helga's observations have particular relevance for the lives of black women, whose servility and self-sacrifice she both admires and abhors. In one exchange with Sary, a mother of six, she wonders how women are able to bear the burdens of all their family and domestic responsibilities. Sary believes that one must simply trust in the "savior" to be delivered in the afterlife. This recurring theme of suffering, female self-sacrifice and deferment repels Helga, ultimately leading her to conclude that there is no God.

Larsen, as well as writers like Zora Neale Hurston and Alice Walker, provided a black feminist humanist context for rejection of organized religion and Christianity that don't rely on revisionist acceptance or soft pedaling of the Bible's brutal misogyny. Larsen's critique is achingly relevant in the midst of an antifeminist backlash that has been partly fueled by the Religious Right and the global regime of corporate media. The emergence of antiabortion fetal "civil rights" laws, the proliferation of hypersexual media imagery promoting violence against women (from rape video games to the sexualization of female preteens in marketing and advertising), and rising HIV/AIDS and STD [sexually transmitted disease] contraction rates among young women of color underscore that women's right to self-determination is increasingly under siege. In mainstream media, popular culture and black communities, black women have been targeted by both Puritanical policing and pornographic fetishization of their sexuality.

Over the past year, black nationalist and black religious organizations have renewed their attacks on abortion and reproductive justice as a form of "black genocide." In some instances they have aligned with the Religious Right on antiabortion billboard campaigns and draconian antiabortion legislation that targets women of color in states like Georgia. These forays once again establish black women's bodies as contested moral battlegrounds. Reproducing more black babies becomes a means of moral and racial redemption. Patriarchal and religious control over black women's bodies is reasserted as the linchpin for black uplift. And in this universe, only race traitor women, in collusion with white supremacist abortion providers, would dare to selfishly "kill" their babies and sacrifice the perpetuation of the race. Good women, on the other hand, learn to sacrifice and be sacrificed. And it is this theme of the good woman that keeps black women dominating the pews and auxiliaries of black churches, while the official face of black church leadership remains male.

The struggle to connect black women's self-determination with the larger issue of human rights enfranchisement is still radical in the 21st-century U.S. And 155 years after the white atheist suffragist abolitionist Ernestine L. Rose was smeared as being "a thousand times, below a prostitute" because of her atheism, feminist humanist non-believers are still in a state of radical moral combat. And in an era in which, to paraphrase black feminist writer Gloria Hull, all of the women "freethinkers" are white, the challenge, for some of us, is to be brave, and to bring the sacrificial good woman out of the closet once and for all.

> *"Roles are important in Judaism. Feminism that seeks total equality of the sexes for the most part rejects that idea of differing roles for men and women."*

Feminism Disparages and Contradicts Orthodox Judaism's Roles for Women

Harry Maryles

Harry Maryles is an Orthodox rabbi from Chicago, Illinois. In the following viewpoint, he discusses the views of Jewish studies author Rebbetzin Tziporah Heller, who has argued that, despite all the social and economic gains made, feminism has fundamentally failed to make women happier because it focuses so strongly on financial and career achievement to the detriment of women who choose to devote themselves to traditional homemaking. According to Heller, the experience of Orthodox women who follow strictly the tenets of Judaism, modern feminism devalues their contributions to society through their families and views them as intellectually inferior. Maryles agrees to a point with Heller, but his argument diverges when it comes to the Jewish notion of separate roles for men and women. According to

Harry Maryles, "Feminism and Judaism—a Double-Edged Sword," Emes Ve-Emunah, 2011. http://haemtza.blogspot.com. Copyright © 2011 by Rabbi Harry Maryles. All rights reserved. Reproduced by permission.

Maryles, feminism has allowed Orthodox women to take on more of the financial burden of families, which in turn allows men to focus more exclusively on their studies—an important function of men in Orthodox culture.

As you read, consider the following questions:

1. According to Maryles, what is the name of the Jewish scripture sung on Friday nights?

2. How does Heller describe her interaction with the Israeli census taker?

3. According to Maryles, what is the name of Heller's sect of Judaism?

I get her point. Rebbetzin Tziporah Heller, a world-renowned author, columnist, teacher, and lecturer on Jewish studies has written an essay at Aish.com that is highly critical of feminism and opens her essay with the following:

> Three decades of feminism have left women with a new version of the quip: If you're so liberated, why aren't you happy?

Her basic thesis is that modern feminism created a society in which women's contributions are largely unrecognized. It's not that she yearns for the pre-feminist ideal of 'the happy homemaker'. Not at all. She is just as critical of 'June Cleaver' as she is of the modern feminist. Her ideal of a Jewish woman is summarized at the end of Mishlei (31:10) that many of us sing on Friday nights before Kiddush Eishes Chayil. As she puts it:

> There we see qualities such as wisdom, courage, creativity, business acumen, and the profound insight to recognize how to relate to individuals according to their specific needs.

I suppose her point is that feminism has destroyed the uniqueness of a Jewish woman and devalued her contributions to home and family, characterizing her role as wife, mother, and homemaker as one of complete ignorance, and stupidity. Her experience with a female census taker in Israel illustrates this quite well:

> Several years ago, the Israeli census taker came to our home. For various reasons I chose not to participate. My children were in school, and the census taker, a woman, found me sitting at the dining room table surrounded by books, looking very professorial. I took time to discuss with her, in Hebrew, my philosophical stance, over a cup of coffee. She was very interested, and left at least respecting my intellectual clarity about my position.
>
> Now, the law requires that anyone refusing to take part in the census must be visited again, so a few weeks later she reappeared. In the meantime, of course, she had interviewed hundreds of people, so she did not recognize me from our previous discussion. This time she saw the Friday morning me. I was surrounded by small children and elbow-deep in challah dough. Surmising my intellectual capacity with a cursory glance at the scene, she pointed at the paper she held and speaking slowly and clearly in beginner's Hebrew said, "This—is—a—census. A—census—is—when—we—count—people. We—want—to—count—ALL—the—people. Sign—this." To her, being a mother and housewife excluded any possibility of my being an intelligent human being.

Has Feminism Created Monsters?

Apparently that census taker defines a woman only by her career and not by her contributions to her family. I must admit that her condescending attitude took me aback. Has feminism really created this monster? Are women who chose to stay home and raise their families all seen as having no intelligence?

What a sad commentary on a movement designed to raise the status of a woman—if she can only be judged by her career. Judaism is not about what we do, but who we are. It isn't about how we make our money that matters—as long as it is done honestly. It is about the content of our character. To have created a mind-set where a homemaker is seen as a person of low intelligence is evidence of a serious failure in the movement. Lest anyone say that this is an aberration of recent vintage, I am reminded of a statement by Hillary Clinton made in March of 1992 when her husband was running for president:

> I suppose I could have stayed home and baked cookies and had teas, but what I decided to do was to fulfill my profession which I entered before my husband was in public life.

Is it any wonder that so many women today value themselves only by what they do career-wise, instead of who they are?

So I definitely think Rebbetzin Heller makes a good point. But her point is only half the story. If one were to read only what she says here, one might conclude that feminism has completely failed the modern woman. And that would be completely false. The truth is quite the opposite.

A New Paradigm

Feminism has contributed mightily to the benefit of all of us, including and perhaps especially the Charedi society of whom I believe Rebbitzin Heller is a part. They are the ones who have shifted the work paradigm from men to women. Men are no longer encouraged to work for a living. They are encouraged to learn full time for as long as possible and to not even think about preparing for a career at all during that time. It is feminism that has enabled them to do that.

Feminism has raised the value of the working, career-oriented woman to the point where she can now earn wages close to her male counterpart. Although disparity still exists and men still mostly get paid more than women for the same work, feminism has enabled Charedi women to support their families—and their husbands in Kollel. Were we to go back to the 'June Cleaver' era, how could the Kollel family possibly survive? That many Kollel men have wives with good jobs that pay a decent salary is what enables them to do what they do.

This phenomenon of better-paying jobs for women in the workplace has not gone unnoticed by Charedi educators. In both America and Israel it is the Charedi woman who is educated towards a career—not the Charedi man.

I recently attended a banquet of a Beis Yaakov where one of their finest Mechanchim extolled their excellent secular curriculum which he said was necessary so that women can better compete in the workplace! Would any of this have been possible without the feminist reality? Hardly.

Rebbetzin Heller in her zeal to paint feminism in a negative light has conveniently ignored the very real contributions it has made to her very own Charedi world.

Not the Whole Story

One has to recognize the truth and not only that part of it that fits with your worldview. In that sense she should have been Makir Tov and recognized the value added to the Charedi world by the very movement she now criticizes for 'masculism'. While her criticism is legitimate, it falls way short of the complete story.

For me feminism is a double-edged sword. It is truly a wonderful phenomenon that has given women the respect they deserve as human beings and has rightfully sought equal pay for equal work. That we are not quite yet there is an outrage that ought to be corrected immediately! But at the same time I also believe that in the social sphere it has gone where it does not belong Jewishly. And it has—at least in some cases—created the kind of monster described above. Rebbetzin Heller is right about that.

Judaism does see women as equal in the eyes of God, but separate from men in how they serve Him. Roles are important in Judaism. Feminism that seeks total equality of the sexes for the most part rejects that idea of differing roles for men and women.

The Tanna R' Meir when asked why he hung out with the 'Tanna turned heretic' Elisha Ben Avuyah, he answered: Tocho Ochel V'Klipaso Zorek. We ought to recognize the contributions of feminism and reject that part of it that contradicts our values.

> *"For me, feminism didn't come about because there's only a problem with Orthodox rabbis. . . . It came about because there's a deep fissure in our community about how we treat different people."*

Feminism and Orthodox Judaism Are Compatible

Kevin D. Grant

Kevin D. Grant is a journalist and an online editor. In the following viewpoint, he interviews Tova Hartman, an Orthodox Jewish leader who runs a feminist synagogue in Jerusalem with congregations in the United States and Canada as well. According to Grant, Hartman's movement is not well accepted by traditional Jewish orthodoxy, in part because it eschews many of the standard Orthodox practices, such as having a hierarchical leadership structure under a single rabbinical leader, allowing women to lead prayer services, and welcoming a wide variety of people to attend, including non-Jews. Many male rabbis, according to Grant, consider Hartman's views and congregation to be an example of the inappropriate application of a radical feminist agenda and would prefer for her to stop her activities or leave Judaism altogether rather than try to introduce change from within. Unlike others in Israel, Grant maintains, Hartman's synagogue receives no state funding and is therefore able to operate as an independent religious community.

As you read, consider the following questions:

1. According to the viewpoint, what is the name of Hartman's congregation?

2. According to the viewpoint, what does Rabbi Asher Lopatin say about Hartman's congregation?

3. What is Hartman's view of the intersection of religion and politics?

Tova Hartman opens the door to her apartment with a warm smile, speaking softly and casually dressed. With her down-to-earth femininity, she doesn't exactly look like a rabble-rouser within Orthodox Judaism.

Which, perhaps, is precisely what makes her so effective.

The 53-year-old psychologist and Jewish scholar has used her decidedly feminist Orthodox synagogue to mount a formidable challenge to the male bastion of religious orthodoxy.

"I don't think that feminism is against the Jewish tradition," she said. "I think it challenges the Jewish tradition."

Nine years ago, Hartman's living room became the first home of Shira Hadasha, a modern Orthodox congregation that now has several hundred members and outposts in the U.S., Canada and Israel. She's one of a handful of rabbis and scholars working to push Orthodox Judaism into a more egalitarian future.

And for the most part, the tradition isn't having it.

"Shira Hadasha came about after trying to change a lot of the local shuls and not succeeding," she said, using the Yiddish word for synagogue. "We understand and accept that our agenda does not resonate yet with modern Orthodox establishment shuls and that's OK. They don't want to change, and they don't have to."

Some Shira Hadasha practices are unusual by Orthodox Jewish standards. The group uses a distributed leadership model. Hartman is not the rabbi—there isn't one—but she is the de facto matriarch. Bat mitzvah ceremonies are available for girls, and women can lead services.

Members emphasize hospitality, welcoming people with disabilities, the elderly, those with mental illness, single mothers and even non-Jews. No one ever leaves Friday night gatherings without a Shabbat dinner to attend.

"Everybody said, 'Nobody has a need for this kind of shul,'" she said. "But the job of the leader is also to create needs."

Separate but Equal?

The Shira Hadasha sanctuary follows the traditional practice of dividing men and women with a separation barrier. But the Torah sits in the center of the room, allowing both men and women to approach it from either side.

"There is," she said, "no back of the bus."

The idea that Shira Hadasha considers itself Orthodox is seen as an anomaly by most within the tradition, making Hartman at once a pariah and a beloved religious leader.

"There are many ways to approach God. I never think there's one way—or one religion," she explained. "I do deeply believe that God listens to different kinds of prayers, but for me (traditional orthodoxy) was untenable."

At times, she has felt trapped by the patriarchy and that her only alternative was to leave. For several years, she abandoned Jewish studies entirely to pursue psychology.

"I know about leaving," she said, looking back. "People would say to me 'If you don't like it, go change it.' What they mean is, 'Go away and change it.' But there's power to staying."

Not surprisingly, many Orthodox rabbis have preferred Hartman had stayed away. Rabbi Yaakov Ariel, the chief rabbi of Tel Aviv's Ramat Gan district, has called Hartman's group "the product of a radical feminist agenda."

"Men who come to the synagogue to pray do not want to be distracted by the prominent appearance of women," Ariel said.

Embracing the Feminine

Yet Hartman's acolytes, including Rabbi Asher Lopatin of Chicago's Anshe Sholom B'nai Israel modern Orthodox synagogue, embrace her teachings, regardless of what the Orthodox hierarchy says.

"Tova is one of my heroes," Lopatin said. "Especially for Orthodoxy, feminism is a foreign, scary concept. But there's a feminine side of men and a feminine side to prayer, and that makes us better Jews."

Hartman said she isn't out to battle her critics, or even try to convince them to change.

"For me, feminism didn't come about because there's only a problem with Orthodox rabbis," she said. "It came about because there's a deep fissure in our community about how we treat different people."

There has been evidence of change in recent years, but it's been slow. Two years ago, Rabbi Avi Weiss and Rabba Sara Hurwitz co-founded Yeshivat Maharat, a rabbinical school for women in New York. But modern Orthodox rabbinical councils have voted to refuse female members, or even acknowledge them as equals.

In Israel, unlike North America, there is no separation between church and state, and the Ministry of Religion funds thousands of synagogues throughout the country. Not surprisingly, Shira Hadasha is not one of them.

Remaining Independent

Yet as an independent community, Hartman's community is able to operate free of many state mandates.

"The matter of religion and politics is where religion goes bad," she said. "I think it's horrible for religion, and it's horrible for the state."

While Hartman supports the idea of the Jewish state and the Israeli law that grants citizenship to Jews who migrate to the Jewish state, she has little patience for Israel's current religious and political leadership.

She particularly laments one impact of Zionism—the historic rift between Jews who believe the Messiah can be hastened by a Jewish return to the Holy Land and those who believe any human attempt to do so is blasphemy—on both Judaism and Israel.

"Zionism broke the Jewish community in half," Hartman said, arguing that Zionism has put ultra-Orthodox traditionalists in charge of Israeli life and religion.

Hartman is the first to acknowledge the limited appeal of her movement, saying she's not sure whether her own daughters are likely to follow in her footsteps.

"Not everybody's clapping," she said. At the same time, "What we're doing has religious integrity."

Periodical and Internet Sources Bibliography

The following articles have been selected to supplement the diverse views presented in this chapter.

Kristin Aune   "Why Feminists Are Less Religious," *Guardian*, March 29, 2011.

Cassandra Balchin   "Jewish. Orthodox. Feminist. Israeli," openDemocracy, April 27, 2011. www .opendemocracy.net.

Amy Clare   "Why Feminism Must Embrace Reason and Shun Religion," *Butterflies and Wheels*, April 28, 2010. www.butterfliesandwheels.org.

Sarah Hamaker   "Christian Women Taking Back 'Feminism,'" The Christian Post, September 8, 2011. www.christianpost.com.

Jo Ellen Green Kaiser   "Do We Still Need Jewish Feminism?," *ZEEK*, June 13, 2011. www.zeek.forward.com.

Shiha Kaur   "Sikhism—a Feminist Religion?," *The F-Word*, April 13, 2010. www.thefword.org.uk.

Lisa Miller   "Evangelical Women Rise as New 'Feminists,'" *Washington Post*, July 28, 2011.

Regan Penaluna   "Christianity and Feminism: Oil and Water?," *First Things*, March 26, 2009. www.first things.com.

Mohammed Wajihuddin   "Burning Burqas and Bras? Nah. Enter the Islamic Feminist," *Times of India*, July 10, 2010.

Sara Yasin   "Muslim Feminist Punk: Helping Destroy Stereotypes of Gender, Religion and Race," AlterNet, February 21, 2011. www.alternet.org.

OPPOSING
VIEWPOINTS®
SERIES

CHAPTER 4

How Are Sexuality and Reproductive Rights Affected by Feminism?

Chapter Preface

Feminism in the twenty-first century has opened to include and reconsider many people and issues that second wave feminists of the 1960s and 1970s had excluded or ignored, typically because they did not fit into the agenda of political change to which that generation of activists adhered. More recently, feminists have intentionally courted groups that are outside the mainstream, including lesbians, African Americans, Latinas, the disabled, and even, to a degree, politically conservative women. Subgroups have developed—including socialist feminism, ecofeminism, black feminism, separatist feminism, and queer theory—but the underlying message is largely the same: Existing power structures have to be challenged, changed, or destroyed in order for women to achieve equality.

One group, however, has been consistently kept outside of feminism's doors. Transgendered women have been accused of being pawns of the patriarchy, reinforcing stereotypes about femininity, and being inherently sexist. Radical lesbian feminist scholar Mary Daly voiced her opposition to transsexualism in her 1978 book *Gyn/Ecology: The Metaethics of Radical Feminism*, likening transgendered women to Frankenstein's monster and insisting that transgendered women were merely "feminine persons," not women. Daly's protégé, Janice G. Raymond, published what is widely considered the signature work of anti-transgender bias among feminists, the 1979 work *The Transsexual Empire: The Making of the She-Male*, in which she asserted that "all transsexuals rape women's bodies by reducing the real female form to an artifact, appropriating this body for themselves. . . . Transsexuals merely cut off the most obvious means of invading women, so that they seem noninvasive."

In 1991 the tension between self-described radical feminists and transgendered women grew when a transsexual woman named Nancy Burkholder attended the Michigan Womyn's Music Festival (MWMF), a women-only feminist music festival held annually since 1976 near Hart, Michigan. Burkholder was identified as transgender by festival attendees, and organizers insisted she leave because, by their definition, she was not biologically a woman. The festival then instituted a strict "womyn-born-womyn" policy. In response, the transgendered community set up an annual gathering of their own, Camp Trans, which takes place down the road from the MWMF.

According to Julia Serano in "Rethinking Sexism: How Trans Women Challenge Feminism," "While many lesbian-feminists today will concede that such accusations [of Mary Daly and Janice G. Raymond] are beyond the pale, their unilateral perspective on sexism still leads them to insist that trans women should not be allowed to enter women-only spaces such as MWMF based on the assumption that trans women have experienced male socialization and privilege in the past, and/or because their bodies, personalities and energies still supposedly remain 'male' or 'masculine' on some level." Serano—who is herself a transsexual—notes that MWMF stopped expelling transgendered women in 2006, although the festival maintains its "womyn-born-womyn" policy. Serano writes that she considers this subtle change to represent "a crucial part of any feminist or activist movement: to allow those who have been marginalized, disenfranchised, and excluded to be able to define themselves, and to speak in their own voices about the struggles they face and the way they experience their own lives."

Feminism's contributions to issues related to women's sexual and reproductive rights form the basis of discussion in this chapter of *Opposing Viewpoints: Feminism*. The viewpoints in this chapter debate such concerns as the roles feminists and feminism should and do play in the pro-choice and right-to-life movements and the impact of SlutWalk protest marches on the women's rights agenda and on stereotypical images of women.

"Abortion is not the only issue at stake here, and it is critical to be talking about reproductive rights as a whole framework, not a single issue."

Feminism Should Promote Reproductive Justice as a Human Rights Issue

S.E. Smith

S.E. Smith is a writer and an activist for women's rights and people with disabilities. In the following viewpoint, she argues that the discussion of reproductive rights has been narrowed to the point of being meaningless to many women, including those who are transgendered and disabled. Smith maintains that even the pro-choice side of the abortion debate reveals discriminatory thinking against people of various races, classes, and genders, with Smith noting that many in the pro-choice feminist community are guilty of "cissexism"—the belief that the genders of transgender people are less authentic or matter less than those of non-transgender people. Additionally, Smith points out that reproductive rights are not just about contraception and abortion but, perhaps more importantly, allow women and men to choose when to have children and how to space them; this, Smith argues, is a basic human right. Smith also addresses enforced sterilization in poor and disabled communities as a violation of human rights.

As you read, consider the following questions:

1. How does Smith describe the institutional approach to birth control for disabled people?

2. What groups does Smith say are subject to having children taken away due to alternative lifestyles?

3. According to Smith, what is the state of reproductive justice in certain poor communities?

Reproductive rights is a dominant social issue in the United States right now. No wonder, with an ongoing onslaught against it from almost all political quarters, between the GOP's straight up attempts to make it impossible to access any kind of reproductive health services to pro-life Democrats. Yet, the discussion of reproductive rights seen in most dominant spaces focuses on a very narrow framework and worldview, and is less about full access to reproductive rights and justice than it is about a very specific issue: abortion.

Now, don't get me wrong. I am a huge fan of abortion access, I think it should be safe, legal, and readily accessible for everybody. But abortion is *not* the only issue at stake here, and it is critical to be talking about reproductive rights as a whole framework, not a single issue.

Three key things to take away: Reproductive rights are not just about women. Reproductive rights are not just about abortion. Reproductive rights have tremendous intersections with race, class, sexuality, and disability.

Reproductive Rights Are Not Just About Women

Reproductive rights are a human rights issue. They matter to all human beings, not just women. I'm a genderqueer person.

I still need access to birth control. I still need people to affirm my right to bodily autonomy, which includes the right to determine whether this body will bear children. Likewise, there are men who need access to reproductive health services up to and including abortion.

When this is brought up in dominant spaces, the result is often pushback, and it often smells of 'wait your turn.' There's a reason the transgender community accuses the pro-choice community of engaging in cissexist [excluding transgender people and concerns] rhetoric. In the eagerness to focus on developing catchy, clear slogans, many people are left by the wayside. In a 'march for women's rights,' you're telling the rest of us that we don't belong. Rhetoric matters and it's important; it's this rhetoric that leads many people to conclude that statements like 'abortion is a men's issue too' refer to the desire to control the bodies of other people, when in fact, for some men, abortion is a very personal issue, as in something they may need to access at some point and will have difficulty accessing safely because of cissexist attitudes.

It's harder to come up with catchy inclusive rhetoric. But it matters.

Reproductive Rights Are Not Just About Abortion

Reproductive rights are about the opportunity to choose the timing and spacing of your children, if you want to have children at all. It is about the right to choose to have children. It is about the right to choose to change your mind; it is about the right of people who affirm at age 25 that they do not want children to change their minds at 35 as much as it is about the right to maintain, for your entire life, that, no, you do not want to have children and you do not plan on having any. It is about the right of people to decide that they want to have children *and* careers, and deserve support to do so.

Many of the attacks on reproductive rights are not just attacks on abortion; they are attacks on human rights. The viciousness of the bile reserved for Planned Parenthood reveals not just anti-choicer hatred, but also the genuine belief in some parts of the United States that birth control is abortion, and because abortion is wrong, people should not have access to any kind of family planning services. It is a reflection of the belief that people who get STIs [sexually transmitted infections] are dirty, dirty sluts who deserve cervical cancer. These are not just about abortion, but about human rights, and about the level of venom reserved for the vagina-owning populace.

Securing full access to reproductive rights for everyone perforce includes abortion protections. Focusing on abortion does not guarantee full access to reproductive rights.

Reproductive Rights Have Tremendous Intersections with Race, Class, Sexuality, and Disability

These are not 'side issues' that people should pay lip service to when they have a chance, or address at some point. They are key, critical issues that *must* be addressed in any and all discussions about reproductive rights. Whether or not you are *allowed* to have children can be determined by race, class, sexuality, and disability status. Minority communities have a fundamentally different relationship with the reproductive rights movement than the majority community. Our relationships include not just the fight for bodily autonomy in an oppressive world, but the fight for *basic humanity* within social justice movements, the need to constantly assert our own personhood in a movement that often rejects us or silences us.

Forcible sterilisation for people with disabilities still happens. Institutionalised people may be forcibly put on birth control or subjected to invasive surgeries for the convenience

The Importance of Reproductive Rights for All People

Women's reproductive rights are essential to realizing a wide range of fundamental human rights.

In particular, women's lives, liberty and security, health, autonomy, privacy, equality and nondiscrimination and education, among others, cannot be protected without ensuring that women can determine when, how and whether to bear children, control their bodies and sexuality, access essential sexual and reproductive health information and services, and be free from violence.

There is reciprocity between women's reproductive rights and a larger human rights framework. Just as women's human rights cannot be realized without promoting women's reproductive rights, reproductive rights draw their meaning and force from long-recognized human rights. Together, they form a constructive dialogue about the meaning of human rights, revealing the impact of laws and policies upon women.

Reproductive Rights Are Human Rights,
Center for Reproductive Rights, 2009.
www.reproductiverights.org.

of the facilities they are incarcerated in. Disabled people are told to seek sterilisation (and rewarded for such) when their disabilities are genetic in nature. Our children are taken away; to take just one example, the Abbie Dorn case, which I've been following for several years now, includes discussions like whether someone 'severely disabled' can 'still [be] a mom.' Children are routinely taken from homes of parents with disabilities, solely on the grounds that they are unfit parents by nature of their disabilities.

Children are routinely taken from the homes of gay and lesbian parents. In some states, gay and lesbian parents lack access to parental rights. Let alone more complex family relationships, like poly households. Parents who are out as bisexual, as kinky, as sex workers, can experience tremendous pressure from government agencies that want to take their children away. Their home environments are deemed 'inherently unsafe for children' on the grounds that they are not sufficiently and acceptably heterosexual in nature.

We still have antiabortion groups using racist tactics to undermine reproductive rights. We cannot look at this in a vacuum; we must also look at the history of racism within the reproductive rights movement and the way that has been weaponised by people who oppose reproductive rights. At the same time that the movement made tremendous strides historically, it was also heralded for reducing the numbers of 'undesirables,' which included people of colour (and people with disabilities, and poor people). The Pill, considered a major breakthrough for reproductive rights and a significant advance in the war for bodily autonomy, came at a tremendous cost for populations used in early experiments; communities which predominantly included nonwhite people and people of colour. This is not to say that the reproductive rights movement is irredeemably racist and unsalvageable, but it *is* to say that there is some very complicated historical context here that we must address, acknowledge, and discuss. Some of the leaders heralded as feminist icons were the very same people advocating eradication of 'undesirable' people!

Sterilisation in Poor Communities

Among many others, Cara Kulwicki has covered, extensively, the use of sterilisation to control poor communities, which often have considerable overlap with people of colour, nonwhite people, and people with disabilities. Drug addicts and alcoholics, many of whom are poor, are paid to be sterilised in the

United States. In Chile, HIV-positive women were sterilised without consent. Many reproductive health access programs in the United States aimed at poor people contain incentives for sterilisation, and stop providing coverage like Pap smears after participants are sterilised. Poverty very much determines access to reproductive health services, and the level of care received.

There's a reason many marginalised communities are turning to the term 'reproductive justice,' to describe a holistic approach to human rights that ensures access to *all people* who need *all services*, whether it's support for people who want to have children and may face considerable social obstacles, or safe, confidential abortion services, or sex [education], or anything in between. Organizations like Asian Communities for Reproductive Justice, SisterSong [Women of Color] Reproductive Justice Collective, Native Youth Sexual Health Network, Black Women for Reproductive Justice, and California Latinas for Reproductive Justice are considering reproductive rights as a complex human rights issue with many intersections, and working towards a world with liberation for all. Many of these organizations are active on the ground doing community organising and centre communities with a historic experience of reproductive oppression in their work to make sure our voices are heard, acknowledged, and incorporated into political actions; all of them are run by members of marginalised communities and we are heavily represented among staff and volunteers. Some of them distance themselves from the mainstream feminist community, a community they feel historically, and currently, underserved by, and with good reason. In return, their work is often ignored.

They're bringing the nuance to a complicated discussion, and it's past time for dominant spaces to up their game.

> *"Feminists for Life calls itself a 'nonpartisan organization.'. . . At the same time, the group's policy agenda . . . does not seem to jibe with the playbook supported by [Sarah] Palin or the Tea Party fans who comprise her base."*

Feminists for Life Fails to Support Women's Rights and Interests

Eleanor J. Bader

Eleanor J. Bader is a Brooklyn-based writer who publishes frequently on progressive issues. In the following viewpoint, she maintains that the antiabortion group Feminists for Life has a contradictory and even deceptive message in its simultaneous claims to advance solutions to social problems such as poverty and its apparent support of political candidates with a record of voting against women's best interests. Bader finds that the policy agenda of Feminists for Life appears to be not just antiabortion but anti-contraception, which, says Bader, presents clear problems for women who do not wish to become pregnant, whether or not they are pro-choice or antiabortion. Additionally, Bader contends, the group fails to recognize or admit that some women would choose to have abortions regardless of whether they had the financial means or the help of a partner to raise a child.

As you read, consider the following questions:

1. According to Bader, did Feminists for Life endorse Sarah Palin's run for vice president?

2. According to Bader, how many children in the United States live in poverty?

3. What is some of the legislation that Feminists for Life has worked to enact?

Sarah Palin, on the vice presidential campaign trail in 2008, raised the profile of a previously obscure antiabortion group, Feminists for Life [FFL], by announcing that she herself was an FFL member. The group did not return the favor by endorsing Palin or the Republican ticket, but the group's new prominence reignited debate about whether it's possible to call oneself a feminist while also opposing a woman's right to choose abortion.

Feminists for Life calls itself a "nonpartisan organization" and the FFL website declares that it "welcome(s) all people regardless of political or religious affiliation." At the same time, the group's policy agenda—which includes support for a wide range of government-subsidized services for pregnant women and children—does not seem to jibe with the playbook supported by Palin or the Tea Party fans who comprise her base.

That said, it is opposition to abortion that gives FFL its reason for being. And while the definition of feminism continues to vex both activists and scholars, many argue that the right to abortion is a central tenet of feminism; that women's liberation rests on a foundation of full reproductive options. FFL believes the opposite, arguing that being "pro-life" (that is, antiabortion) is inextricably linked to female empowerment.

FFL was founded in 1972, a year before *Roe v. Wade*, the U.S. Supreme Court ruling that gave women the legal right to end unwanted pregnancies. The organization's founders were two members of the National Organization for Women [NOW] who agreed with NOW's agenda—except for its support of liberalized abortion. Unable to convince NOW to retract its abortion rights platform, they created FFL to oppose abortion while pushing for the social safety net they believed was necessary to make having a child a viable option. This dual purpose has spurred FFL's work ever since and Cayce Utley, FFL's national program director—formerly a staff person at Democrats for Life of America, which describes itself as "the pro-life voice and wing of the Democratic Party"—is quick to state that even if *Roe* is eventually overturned, the group will still have "a lot of work to do in changing the way families are received by society."

The Social Safety Net Is Badly Damaged

Indeed, the fact that nearly 40 million Americans, including one in five children under 18, live in poverty indicates how much needs to be done to address the economic disparities that exist throughout the United States. For Feminists for Life, this means working to improve access to benefits supporting healthy families, from increased welfare benefits to increased child care options for low- and middle-income households. FFL'S website champions a raft of important—and decidedly not Tea Partyish—pro-family policies: Expanded educational opportunities for poor students; additional employment options for women; micro loans and business assistance for would-be entrepreneurs; low-cost health care before, during, and after the birth of a child; clean water; assistance for women trying to leave physically violent or emotionally abusive partners; and support for housing subsidies.

What's more, FFL was the only anti-choice group to work alongside NOW, NARAL [Pro-Choice America], and the Feminist Majority to push for such legislation as the Violence Against Women Act, the Equal Rights Amendment, the State Children's Health Insurance Program, and the Family and Medical Leave Act. Most recently, the group campaigned for the Elizabeth Cady Stanton Pregnant and Parenting Student Services Act, approved by Congress this year, which, beginning in 2011, will provide a total of $25 million a year to states for the establishment of services for pregnant students and school-age parents.

In addition, the group has launched an aggressive program on college campuses. According to Utley, FFL will send a speaker—fees range from $1,000–$3,000 a pop—to campuses anywhere in the country, or will assist women's groups in organizing rallies and petition drives to demand better resources for students who are pregnant or parenting. "Our goal is to change campus culture, to include resources for students who are about to start a family," Utley says. "In some colleges the message is pretty clear—have an abortion or your college experience is over. At the same time, we're fighting against the remnants of higher education that were originally designed to meet the needs of affluent white men."

But if increasing resources so that young parents don't have to drop out of school sounds like a no-brainer, that's because it's something that reproductive justice activists have been saying—albeit with a pro-choice caveat—since the late 1970s: Women have the right to decide when and whether to have a child and should have access to whatever they need to do so, whether it's a Medicaid-funded abortion or nutritious food.

Some Women Will Still Choose Abortion

And therein lies the conflict between pro-choice feminists and those, like FFL members, who oppose abortion. At the crux of the issue is FFL's refusal to accept that some women will want to end a pregnancy even when they have the economic re-

sources to have a child and even when they have a partner with whom to share responsibilities. FFL members further deny that many women see abortion as a relief and not a last resort.

Carol Hornbeck, a marriage and family therapist with a master's degree from Christian Theological Seminary in Indianapolis, sees this blind spot as an oversimplification of reality: "Solutions don't have to be black or white," she says. "If you believe in the core value of life as sacred, to be protected, you have to engage with the grey areas. Humans have free will and sometimes you have to acknowledge that one person's needs will come into conflict with another person's needs. We have the power to choose and sometimes that means a woman places her own physical, mental, emotional, and spiritual well-being above the needs of a fertilized egg."

Not surprisingly, you won't see or hear that tension, that conflict, if you talk to FFL or peruse their materials. Several FFL videos, for example, make a compelling case for choosing childbirth over abortion. *Chauncie's Journey*, for one, tells the story of Chauncie Saelins Brusie—now an FFL staffer—who became pregnant during her senior year of college. Her emotional account describes a university bureaucracy that was unprepared for her decision to continue her pregnancy. Maternity coverage was not provided by the school health plan she'd purchased and there were neither family dorms nor child care facilities on campus. "I understand the sheer panic that could lead a woman to abortion," Chauncie says in the film. Her ultimate decision to marry her boyfriend and bear the child is told with passion and genuine feeling. What's missing is the realization that Chauncie made the choice that was right for her, a choice that might be completely wrong for someone else.

Joyce Ann McCauley-Benner stars in another of FFL's heartrending videos. She begins by describing her journey from home to a college 1,100 miles from where she grew up. Working two jobs to support herself, she looks directly into the camera to describe being raped by a coworker and subsequently learning that she was pregnant. "I felt unready to be a mom," she confesses. "I had no health insurance and was in a daze." Then, after weeks of grappling with what to do, she decided to have the baby. "I realized that I knew who the mother was and there was as much of me inside this baby as there was of the rapist," she says.

There's no way to argue with [McCauley-]Benner's decision and all viewers can do is hope that she never regrets her choice. It's poignant stuff, but the equally poignant reality that other women have no desire to bear the child of a rapist—let alone raise it or place it for adoption—seems lost on [McCauley-]Benner and FFL.

Contraception: Mixed Messages and Misinformation

Then there's the issue of birth control, a subject Feminists for Life both skirts and subtly discourages. According to the FFL website, "There is no FFL position on contraception except when it presents a threat to women's health. Some FFL members support the use of contraception as long as there is no abortifacient [an agent that induces abortion] effect, while others oppose it. Some oppose all forms of contraception for health reasons, others for religious reasons. Others prefer natural methods to plan a family."

On the subject of emergency contraception, aka "Plan B" or the "morning-after pill" [a drug that disrupts fertilization], the website refers readers to Optionline.org—a misnomer if there ever was one—that blatantly discourages the use of the drug. Full of misinformation, the site includes erroneous statements such as this: "You can only become pregnant on certain days of the month—around the time you ovulate." The site also resorts to scare tactics, contending, for instance, that "Taking the morning-after pill at a time when you cannot become pregnant needlessly exposes you to large doses of hormones. If you are already pregnant from an earlier sexual encounter taking the morning-after pill is of no value and may cause harm."

FFL has also been criticized for distorting history in the service of its anti-choice agenda. To wit, the group contends that the 19th-century founders of the women's movement were unequivocally against abortion. "Women deserve better than abortion," their website states, and "those who walk in the shoes of early American feminists such as Elizabeth Cady

Stanton are invited to call FFL home." FFL member Carol Crossed recently purchased the Adams, Massachusetts, birthplace of Stanton's colleague, Susan B. Anthony, and turned it into a museum. But even though the group calls Anthony an antiabortion foremother, a host of historians—including staff at the Susan. B. Anthony Center for Women's Leadership at the University of Rochester and Anthony scholars Lynn Sherr and Ann Gordon—have contested this interpretation of Anthony's position.

Social Welfare vs. Abortion Access

FFL has come under further fire for honoring conservative antiabortion blogger and syndicated columnist Michelle Malkin, whose writing is contemptuous of virtually every social initiative that FFL claims to hold dear. And even though FFL did not endorse Sarah Palin's vice presidential run, the fact that the group has never criticized her political wish list makes one question whether their purported support of pro-family initiates in somehow negotiable. Indeed, this omission has prompted pro-choice feminists to wonder if FFL is willing to jettison its laudable social welfare agenda in exchange for support of policies that will curtail abortion access.

"We're not a political action committee," National Program Director Cayce Utley says. "Anyone can join FFL without a political litmus test and some people on board with us are conservative and others are liberal. We're an education and advocacy group. Our aim is to educate pro-lifers to our point of view, what we think it means to be a pro-life feminist. We try to help people connect the dots between supporting policies that help pregnant women raise healthy children and seeing that if they don't support public welfare programs, women will likely make decisions about pregnancy that they won't like."

As for feminism, Utley concedes that the word's meaning has become increasingly murky. Does that matter? I ask her.

"Feminists for Life walks the talk," she says. "We support progressive solutions for women and families."

Maybe it comes down to the word progressive, and whether pro-family solutions can be deemed progressive if they demonize abortion—something women opt for whether the procedure is legal or not, despite FFL blather to the contrary, because not every child is wanted—and dance around the efficacy of birth control. The world may change, and language, too, but one thing remains obvious: The onus is on FFL to assess Palin's platform—and that of Tea Party activists across the country—and call them what they are: Anti-woman, anti-poor, anti-worker programs that are wholly antithetical to the interests of most U.S. families.

> "Many women . . . are attracted . . . to the message of groups like Feminists for Life, which tells women facing unplanned pregnancies that they should 'refuse to choose' between having a future and having a baby."

Young Women Embrace Feminists for Life's Antiabortion Agenda as Empowering

Colleen Carroll Campbell

Colleen Carroll Campbell is a radio host and an author who writes about matters related to Christianity. In the following viewpoint, she argues that antiabortion feminism is on the rise, attracting increasing numbers of young women who are frustrated with the pro-choice movement's stringency. According to Campbell, feminists who say they are pro-choice fail to protect the rights of women and girls by allowing for no alternatives to their agenda, refusing even to condemn sex-selective abortion. Campbell finds that Feminists for Life appeals to women who believe that pro-choice policies fail to respect women's dignity and who interpret the pro-choice philosophy as a failure to support women of childbearing age. Campbell cites polls that have found that an increasing number of women, particularly young women, identify as "pro-life" or "strongly pro-life." Campbell finds that pro-choice feminism lacks the "youthful enthusiasm" of its antiabortion cohort, concluding that the dispute will open the doors for a redefinition of the meaning of "feminism."

As you read, consider the following questions:

1. What does Campbell say the Overbrook Research poll in Missouri showed about women's stance on abortion?

2. According to Campbell, what are the two demographic groups most likely to believe abortion should be outlawed?

3. According to Campbell, how did NARAL Pro-Choice America president Nancy Keenan describe abortion-rights supporters?

Can you be a feminist and oppose abortion in all circumstances? Can you be a person of faith and support abortion in some circumstances?

The very notion of pro-life feminism is an affront to the vociferous leaders of America's abortion-rights lobby and the aging ranks of its feminist establishment—two groups that are, for all practical purposes, indistinguishable. The overlap between these two groups and their shared indignation at organizations like Feminists for Life and women like [2008 vice presidential candidate] Sarah Palin is no accident. It is a consequence of their decades-long campaign to make feminism synonymous with a woman's right to abort her child and to marginalize any freethinking feminist who dares to disagree.

We hear a lot about the absolutism of women like Palin, who opposes abortion even in the hard cases. Often overlooked is the absolutism of her critics—avowedly "pro-woman" abortion-rights advocates who cannot bring them-

Pro-Life Feminism Is Pro-Woman

Feminists for Life, like [Susan B.] Anthony and our other feminist foremothers, recognizes that abortion is a reflection that our society has failed to meet the needs of women. In response, we are dedicated to systematically eliminating the root causes that drive women to abortion—primarily lack of practical resources and support—through holistic, woman-centered solutions. We promote the resources women want and need to make nonviolent choices, and our own efforts are shaped by the core feminist values of justice, nondiscrimination, and nonviolence.

Cat Clark, "The Truth About Susan B. Anthony:
Did One of America's First Feminists Oppose Abortion?,"
The American Feminist, *Spring 2007.*

selves to condemn even partial-birth or sex-selective abortion, the latter of which is an increasingly common practice in the U.S. and abroad in which unborn girls are targeted for elimination simply because they are girls.

For many American women, the feminism that once attracted them with its lofty goal of promoting respect for women's dignity has morphed into something antithetical to that dignity: a movement that equates a woman's liberation with her license to kill her unborn child, marginalizes people of faith if they support even modest restrictions on abortion, and colludes with a sexist culture eager to convince a woman in crisis that dealing with her unplanned pregnancy is her choice and, therefore, her problem.

Defending Dignity

Many women are not buying it. They are attracted instead to the message of groups like Feminists for Life, which tells women facing unplanned pregnancies that they should "refuse to choose" between having a future and having a baby. They believe that the best way for a woman to defend her own dignity is to defend the dignity of each and every human person, including the one that grows within her womb. And they reject the false dichotomy of abortion-centric feminism that says respect for human dignity is a zero-sum game in which a woman can win only if her unborn child loses.

This rising pro-life sentiment among women has begun to surface in public opinion polls. A 2007 study from Overbrook Research tracked the abortion views of women in Missouri, considered to be a bellwether [an indicator of trends] state on such issues. Researchers found that the share of Missouri women identifying themselves as "strongly pro-life" rose from 28 percent in 1992 to 37 percent in 2006, with the ranks of the "strongly pro-choice" shrinking from about a third to a quarter of Missouri women. This pro-life shift was even more pronounced among young women.

More recent studies show similar results. A Gallup poll taken last May [2009] found that, for the first time since Gallup began asking the question in 1995, a majority of Americans now identify themselves as "pro-life" rather than "pro-choice." Gallup found a significant rise in the percentage of young adults who believe that abortion should be illegal in all circumstances, from about one in seven in the early 1990s to one in four today. Eighteen- to 29-year-olds are now tied with seniors as the group most likely to favor the outlawing of abortion.

Abortion-rights activists have noticed this trend, and it worries them. A few weeks ago, *Newsweek* published an article in which NARAL [Pro-Choice America] president Nancy Keenan described her fellow abortion-rights crusaders as members of the "postmenopausal militia." She noted with concern that the youthful enthusiasm in the abortion debate seems to be on the pro-life side. Upon seeing the swarms of hundreds of thousands of participants at this year's [2010's] March for Life in Washington, D.C., many of them motivated equally by religious faith and concern for human rights, Keenan said: "I just thought, my gosh, they are so young. There are so many of them, and they are so young."

Indeed, they are. They are young, their ranks are growing, and the girls and women among them are not buying yesterday's orthodoxy about the inextricable link between abortion and women's liberation. No matter how many times the feminist establishment tells them to sit down and shut up, they show no signs of doing so. Let the debate over the true meaning of feminism begin.

> *"The rejection by women of compulsory cleansing of mind, body, and soul is a necessary pre-condition of liberation."*

SlutWalks Discourage Sexual Violence by Demanding Sexual Freedom

Germaine Greer

Germaine Greer is an Australian scholar and feminist and the author of the seminal feminist 1970 classic The Female Eunuch. *In the following viewpoint, she offers a strongly supportive argument for "SlutWalks," which became a major subject of controversy among feminists in 2011, when the marches were instituted as a movement to protest rape and remove the blame and scrutiny from women who have been raped. Greer explains the historical meaning of the word "slut" as a dirty, slovenly woman, usually a kitchen maid, and compares this view of an entire class of women with the twentieth-century housewife who was encouraged to keep her house as clean as possible and was, in the process, also metaphorically connected to dirt and treated as second class. Taken together, according to Greer, these two types of women give the young feminists reason to take to the streets in protest.*

As you read, consider the following questions:

1. According to Greer, how did SlutWalks originate?

2. What, according to Greer, are SlutWalkers trying to "reclaim"?

3. What does Greer say women must become more tolerant of in order to liberate themselves?

The Toronto policeman who in January [2011] told a "personal security class" at York University that "women should avoid dressing like sluts in order not to be victimised" said nothing unusual. What made news was what happened 10 weeks later, when a thousand people hit the streets of downtown Toronto in a "slut walk".

That was surprising, but not as surprising as what happened next. Within days, all over North America, in Britain and even in Australia, women came together to organise slut walks of their own. Throughout the English-speaking world, it seems there are hordes of women prepared to sashay round the streets provocatively dressed, making a defiant display of their inner slut.

The mind police were not amused. The most sanctimonious of our newspapers solemnly intoned that "women need to take to the streets to condemn violence, but not for the right to be called 'slut'". But it was not heeded. The women (and men) who are set to prance the streets of dozens of cities in underwear and fetish gear for weeks to come will be taking liberties. That's where liberation begins.

Slut-walkers are apt to say that the purpose of their action is to "reclaim the word". It's difficult, probably impossible, to

SlutWalks Reflect Contemporary Feminist Activism and Ideals

In a feminist movement that is often fighting simply to hold ground, SlutWalks stand out as a reminder of feminism's more grassroots past and point to what the future could look like. . . .

The success of SlutWalks does herald a new day in feminist organizing. One when women's anger begins on-line but takes to the street, when a local step makes global waves and when one feminist action can spark debate, controversy and activism that will have lasting effects on the movement.

Jessica Valenti,
"SlutWalks and the Future of Feminism,"
Washington Post, *June 3, 2011.*

reclaim a word that has always been an insult. And yet here are women spontaneously deciding to adopt it. Before we decide that thousands of our sisters are simply stupid or misguided, an attempt must be made to understand what's going on. The slut walk manifesto states: "Historically, the term 'slut' has carried a predominantly negative association. Aimed at those who were sexually promiscuous, be it for work or pleasure, it has primarily been women who have suffered under the burden of this label. We are tired of being oppressed by slut-shaming; of being judged by our sexuality. . . ."

The Historical Meaning of "Slut"

A little knowledge here misleads. Historically, the primary attribute of a slut is not promiscuity but dirt. The word denotes a "woman of dirty, slovenly, or untidy habits or appearance; a foul slattern". A now obsolete meaning connects it with a kitchen maid, whose life was lived in soot and grease. She was too dirty to be allowed above stairs, but drudged out her painful life scraping pans and riddling ash, for 16 hours a day, and then retreated to her squalid lodging where hot water could not be had. The corner she left un-swept was the slut corner; the fluff that collected under the furniture was a slut ball. People who thought of sex as dirt suspected the lazy kitchen maid of being unclean in that way as well.

If the kitchen maid's life was made wretched by the struggle against dirt, the life of the housewife was hardly less so. A woman who didn't hang out her washing when everyone else did, who didn't scrub her front doorstep and windowsills, who didn't scour everything that could be scoured at least once a week, but preferred to gossip with her friends or play with her children in the sun, would also be suspected of being no better than she should be. A man married to a sloven needed to take her in hand if he was not to be generally despised.

The Modern-Day Aversion to "Dirty" Women

Twenty-first century women are even more relentlessly hounded and harassed by the threat of dirt. No house is ever clean enough, no matter how many hours its resident woman spends spraying and wiping, Hoovering, dusting, disinfecting and deodorising. Women's bodies can never be washed often enough to be entirely free of dirt; they must be depilated and deodorised as well. When it comes to sex, women are as dirty as the next man, but they don't have the same right to act out their fantasies. If they're to be liberated, women have to demand the right to be dirty. By declaring themselves sluts, they lay down the Cillit Bang [a brand of cleaning products] and take up the instruments of pleasure.

Men already enjoy the right to be dirty. In the usual rugby house, unwashed dishes can be found festering under beds as well as piled to chin height in the sink. The rubbish bin will contain an impacted mess of stomped-down rubbish. The lavatory would be only too accurately described as a bog. The filth becomes a challenge; the first man to crack and grab the Hoover is a sissy. In mixed digs in our tolerant universities, it's the women who are forever cleaning the shared facilities, because the men won't. The con is a simple one. If you don't mind that the toilet's disgusting, then don't clean it; if you do, then do. Girls don't have the option of not minding. Dirty house equals dirty woman equals tramp.

If women are to overthrow the tyranny of perpetual cleansing, we have to be able to say: "Yes, I am a slut. My house could be cleaner. My sheets could be whiter. I could be without sexual fantasies too—pure as the untrodden snow—but I'm not. I'm a slut and proud." The rejection by women of compulsory cleansing of mind, body and soul is a necessary pre-condition of liberation. Besides, taking part in what looks like an endless "vicars and tarts" street party is not just bad-ass. It's fun.

> *"Feminists are supposed to be counter-cultural, yet by marching in fishnets and bras with the word 'slut' scrawled on their bodies, they are simply imitating a culture that objectifies and hyper-sexualizes women and girls."*

SlutWalks Demean Women and Encourage Sexual Objectification

Kirsten Powers

Kirsten Powers is a political analyst and a columnist for the Daily Beast. In the following viewpoint, she contends that Slut-Walks are misguided and demeaning and will ultimately harm women because they uphold the very characteristics of the culture they are trying to subvert. According to Powers, many women who have worked in prostitution are offended by Slut-Walks, and some feminists would prefer the SlutWalkers to protest the kind of rape that they say is common in prostitution and pornography rather than trying to put a humorous spin on female sexuality, as supporters of the SlutWalks say they are doing. Feminists engaged in the dispute over SlutWalks, says Powers, generally fall into either the liberal vein of women who support pornography and prostitution as sex work that deserves to be dignified or radical feminists who believe all such sex work is necessarily exploitative and dangerous.

As you read, consider the following questions:

1. According to Powers, how many SlutWalks were planned around the world as of the date of her writing?

2. At what age does Powers say the average boy begins viewing online pornography?

3. What does Powers quote Gail Dines as saying about the message men who observe SlutWalks will receive?

D id you hear about the feminist fund-raiser that was held at a Washington, D.C., strip club?

No, I'm not making that up. It gets better: They were raising money for an event called "SlutWalk DC," which is part of a growing "movement" that is popping up all over the world.

It started when a police officer in Toronto told some students at a campus safety meeting that in order to avoid being victimized, women "should avoid dressing like sluts." There have already been SlutWalks in Toronto, Boston, and Dallas, with more than 20 planned from Sydney to Buenos Aires to Seattle. The stated purpose of the SlutWalks is to stop blaming victims for rapes and to "reclaim the word slut." The former is a laudable goal; the latter not just naïve but also harmful to women.

Feminists are supposed to be countercultural, yet by marching in fishnets and bras with the word "slut" scrawled on their bodies, they are simply imitating a culture that objectifies and hypersexualizes women and girls on a scale never before seen in history. Thanks to mass media, we now are inundated with movies, music videos, magazines, porn sites, and billboards that all send the same message: Women are there

Cultural Sexualization of Girls Begins Early

Doll play is a popular activity for children, especially girls. It is therefore of concern when sexualized dolls are marketed to girls. One series of dolls popular with girls as young as age 4 are the Bratz dolls, a multiethnic crew of teenagers who are interested in fashion, music, boys, and image. Bratz girls are marketed in bikinis, sitting in a hot tub, mixing drinks, and standing around, while the "Boyz" play guitar and stand with their surf boards, poised for action. Moreover, Bratz dolls come dressed in sexualized clothing such as miniskirts, fishnet stockings, and feather boas. Although these dolls may present no more sexualization of girls or women than is seen in MTV videos, it is worrisome when dolls designed specifically for 4- to 8-year-olds are associated with an objectified adult sexuality. The objectified sexuality presented by these dolls, as opposed to the healthy sexuality that develops as a normal part of adolescence, is limiting for adolescent girls, and even more so for the very young girls who represent the market for these dolls.

"Report of the APA Task Force on the Sexualization of Girls,"
American Psychological Association, 2010. www.apa.org.

for your ogling and consumption. The average age a boy starts looking at online porn—which often sexualizes abuse and humiliation of women—is 11.

SlutWalk organizers say dressing up like the "sluts" that most men would associate with their favorite porn star is meant to be ironic, and even funny. Which prompts a question: Have they ever met any men? Do they really think that when men see scantily clad women holding signs saying "Slut Pride," the first thing they think of is women's empowerment?

The Response of Prostitutes

In Boston, a bunch of Neanderthals threatened to hold a "pimp walk" in response to the SlutWalk. Rebecca Mott, a former prostitute and activist who is horrified by the Slut-Walks, told me, "The Australian Sex Party actually said we could hand out packs where men can hide their hands where they are wanking themselves at the SlutWalks."

Mott, a Brit who barely survived the hellish nightmare of her life as a prostitute, tried to convince the feminist organizer of the London SlutWalk of the damage she was doing, only to be patronized and shushed. "For women who are forced to wear those clothes because they are sold and bought to see other people dressed up like that for laughs and to say it's 'liberating' is really hard to take," she says.

Aura Bogado, an Argentinean feminist and Yale student who took to her blog to blast the SlutWalk organizers, told me: "It's like a minstrel show. They pretend to live the experience [Rebecca] lived." As she blogged, the SlutWalk event "highlights its origins from a privileged position of relative power, replete with an entitlement of assumed safety that women of color [like me] would never even dream of. We do not come from communities in which it feels at all harmless to call ourselves 'sluts.'"

Mott wrote on her blog, "If you want to feel good about stopping rapes, it would be cool if you could end the institutionalized, common and usually sadistic rapes of women and girls in porn and prostitution. I want marches demanding an end to the sex trade, marches saying prostitution is to pay-to-rape, marches speaking out about the sadism in the production of porn."

Don't hold your breath.

Pro-Pornography Feminists

Samantha Wright, the organizer of the D.C. SlutWalk, which held its fund-raiser in a strip club, told me: "I do see how it's hard coming from an anti-porn standpoint to see how Slut-Walks could be beneficial. I consider myself a feminist [who is] pro-pornography. There has to be freedom of choice for women to work in [the sex] industry." She said it was important to her that women in the sex industry "know that we believe in their right to not be sexually assaulted," which is at least one thing on which everyone can agree.

After talking to numerous SlutWalk organizers—all of them bright, sincere women who care deeply about preventing victim-blaming for rape—the common thread was that they were liberal feminists who believe that women in prostitution, stripping, and pornography are doing "sex work" by choice, whereas Mott and women who align themselves with radical feminism believe it's just old-fashioned slavery.

Gail Dines, professor of women's studies at Boston's Wheelock College and author of *Pornland: How Porn Has Hijacked Our Sexuality*, finds the SlutWalks alarming. She told me, "It is not understanding the context of the world they are living in. The average male today gets his major sex education from porn. And the message they get is that women are sluts." To the liberal feminists, whom Dines calls porn and prostitution apologists, she asks: "If it's such a great profession, why aren't you turning tricks?"

Megan Walker, executive director of the London Abused Women's Centre in London, Ontario, told me that the women embracing the SlutWalks "are definitely part of a movement that has been influenced by a rape and porn culture. Women who come into the center talk about how they are forced to dress up like the porn star and what a big role it has played in their rapes by intimate partners."

Mott says the SlutWalkers are playing "slut" for kicks, while women and girls trapped in the sex industry—or those being sexually abused at home, as she says she was by her stepfather—are forced to be what she calls the "ultimate slut" with little hope for escape.

Dines dismisses as ludicrous the idea that men who consume porn typically based on the idea that the "slut is getting what she deserves" would see these walks as anything more than a public peep show. "There is no way [those men] are going to get the joke. The joke is on us. It's on women."

Periodical and Internet Sources Bibliography

The following articles have been selected to supplement the diverse views presented in this chapter.

Denise Balkissoon	"Sex in the City: An Interview with Jessica Yee," *Eyeweekly*, February 23, 2011.
Kelly J. Bell	"A Feminist's Argument on How Sex Work Can Benefit Women," *Student Pulse*, November 2, 2009.
Brendan Carroll	"Feminism, Porn and Dignity," *Daily Princetonian*, April 30, 2010.
Petra de Vries	"From Slave to Sex Worker," *L'Homme*, January 2010.
Megan Gibson	"Will SlutWalks Change the Meaning of the Word *Slut*?," *Time*, August 12, 2011.
Jennifer Hartline	"Opinion: 'Feminists' and Abortion: Real Feminism Does Not Kill!," Catholic Online, July 6, 2010. www.catholic.org.
Kate Morris	"The Harlot's Curse: Feminism and Prostitution," *Fringe Magazine*, February 8, 2007. www.fringemagazine.org.
Deborah Orr	"Feminists Shouldn't Try to Stifle Debate About Abortion," *Guardian*, May 25, 2011.
Nina Power	"10 Things That Feminism Could Do Better," AlterNet, July 9, 2010. www.alternet.org.
Harsha Walia	"Slutwalk—To March or Not to March," Rabble.ca, May 8, 2011. http://rabble.ca.

For Further Discussion

Chapter 1

1. Annie Lennox and the other women who participated in the roundtable discussion on feminism agree that their generation of women growing up in Western countries has benefited immensely from second wave feminism's legal and social advancements, but they maintain that sexism has taken more insidious forms in the period after second wave feminism. What are some of these more insidious forms, and do you agree or disagree?

2. Christina Hoff Sommers argues that the feminist movement of the 1960s and 1970s performed successfully and has become irrelevant, particularly in recent years when economic realities have created an increasingly difficult financial environment for American men, who, Sommers suggests, might be in need of a movement of their own. What do you think of her assessment? Does it seem to you that economic conditions for men in the twenty-first century merit the kind of movement women had in the twentieth century?

3. Jessica Valenti argues that feminists have inadvertently diminished the stature of feminism by positioning gender as the single issue upon which they choose to focus as a dividing factor in the United States. Valenti cites Gloria Steinem's controversial 2008 editorial in which Steinem wrote that gender continues to be the single greatest factor restricting American citizens from achievement. Do you think Valenti places Steinem in her proper context within the twentieth-century feminist movement? Do you think it is possible for second and third wave feminists to understand one another?

Chapter 2

1. Lisa Solod writes about Michele Bachmann's commitment to Christian "dominionism," which holds that wives must submit to their husbands according to biblical principles. Do you think dominionism contradicts the separation of church and state? Why or why not?

2. Meredith Tax maintains that feminists were divided during the 2008 presidential election between those who believe that gender alone should be considered in questions of women's equality and those who believe that gender is only one factor in a wider span of issues including race, class, and disability. Do you think this division is related to a generational divide between women? Why or Why not?

3. Amanda Fortini discusses the sexism in American culture that was exposed by the treatment of Hillary Clinton during the 2008 presidential election, quoting women from a broad spectrum of high-earning careers who say they have encountered blatant sexism in their work. Do you think women should expect a certain amount of sexism from men? Are a high income and a position of power fair trades in some careers? Explain your position.

4. Hanna Rosin suggests that the Tea Party has allowed many women, who otherwise would not have had the opportunity, to aspire to positions of power in political office. Do you believe it is accurate for conservative Christian women in the Tea Party to call themselves feminists? Can a woman be a feminist even if she does not believe some of the traditional core principles of feminism?

Chapter 3

1. According to Amina Wadud, Islam has been misinterpreted by patriarchy, and Islamic feminists must return to the original source material to reinterpret the role of women within Muslim culture in a more equitable man-

ner. Do you think it is possible to be both a Muslim and a feminist given patriarchal interpretations of the Quran? Can Islamic feminists redefine their religion?

2. Caroline B. Glick maintains that liberal feminists in Western countries ignore abuses of women under Islam. Do you think Glick is right about such "political correctness," or do you think the abuses Glick lists, such as honor killings, are openly discussed by Western observers? Given Amina Wadud's assertion that Islamic feminists can and should change Islam from within, do you think Western influence would make a difference?

3. Mimi Haddad and Kathryn Joyce offer very different views of Christianity's approach to women and feminism. Do you think the two views of women are equally represented in modern Christianity? What do you think accounts for Quiverfull's popularity?

4. Sikivu Hutchinson discusses how African American Christian women have been coerced into a life of personal sacrifice. What parallels, if any, do you see between this model of womanhood within that form of Christianity and the Quiverfull movement described by Kathryn Joyce?

Chapter 4

1. Eleanor J. Bader states that Feminists for Life's position as simultaneously antiabortion and anti-contraception is hypocritical. Do you find the position contradictory? Why or why not?

2. Colleen Carroll Campbell cites evidence that many young women identify themselves as "pro-life" or "strongly pro-life" and maintains that pro-choice feminists are overly concerned with ideology, to the point where they will even reject restrictions on sex-specific abortion, causing female fetuses to be aborted. Do you think this is a legitimate concern for feminists?

3. SlutWalks are one of the most controversial new forms of protest among third wave feminists. Do you think both sides have valid points, or is one argument stronger than the other?

Organizations to Contact

The editors have compiled the following list of organizations concerned with the issues debated in this book. The descriptions are derived from materials provided by the organizations. All have publications or information available for interested readers. The list was compiled on the date of publication of the present volume; the information provided here may change. Be aware that many organizations take several weeks or longer to respond to inquiries, so allow as much time as possible.

American Association of University Women (AAUW)
1111 Sixteenth Street NW, Washington, DC   20036
(202) 785-7700
e-mail: connect@aauw.org
website: www.aauw.org

The American Association of University Women (AAUW) has existed for more than 120 years to increase access to higher education for women and girls and to ensure gender equity in institutions of higher learning. The group publishes research on various issues that affect women and girls, offers grants and fellowships, and maintains leadership programs.

Association of Reproductive Health Professionals (ARHP)
1901 L Street NW, Suite 300, Washington, DC   20036
(202) 466-3825 • fax: (202) 466-3826
e-mail: arhp@arhp.org
website: www.arhp.org

The Association of Reproductive Health Professionals (ARHP) is a multidisciplinary organization for members of the medical profession, health educators, researchers, and reproductive health policy makers that focuses on offering continuing education for reproductive health professionals. ARHP offers accreditation for members, publishes research papers, and advocates for policy changes.

Center for Reproductive Rights (CRR)
120 Wall Street, New York, NY   10005
(917) 637-3600 • fax: (917) 637-3666
e-mail: info@reprorights.org
website: http://reproductiverights.org

The Center for Reproductive Rights (CRR) is an organization of attorneys and activists focused on strengthening reproductive rights legislation throughout the United States and internationally. CRR has brought cases before state and district courts, the US Supreme Court, United Nations committees, and regional human rights groups, using international human rights law, the US Constitution, and the Universal Declaration of Human Rights as the basis for its arguments.

Feminist Majority Foundation (FMF)
1600 Wilson Boulevard, Suite 801, Arlington, VA   22209
(703) 522-2214 • fax: (703) 522-2219
e-mail: media@feminist.org
website: http://feminist.org

Founded in 1987, the Feminist Majority Foundation (FMF) engages in research and public policy development to increase gender equity in areas such as employment and pay, reproductive rights, legal and political representation, and education. Additionally, the group provides leadership training for young feminists and works in conjunction with its sister organization, Feminist Majority, which uses direct political action and lobbying to influence policy.

NARAL Pro-Choice America
1156 Fifteenth Street NW, Suite 700, Washington, DC   20005
(202) 973-3000 • fax: (202) 973-3096
website: www.prochoiceamerica.org

NARAL Pro-Choice America is a political advocacy group that lobbies for reproductive rights and legal abortion access through state and federal chapters throughout the United States.

National Hispana Leadership Institute (NHLI)

1601 North Kent Street, Suite 803, Arlington, VA   22209
(703) 527-6007 • fax: (703) 527-6009
website: www.nhli.org

National Hispana Leadership Institute (NHLI) is a nonprofit organization dedicated to training and placing more Latina women in positions of power in the public and private sectors. The organization offers professional development, engages in community activism, and provides mentors and continuing education to young Hispanic women.

National Latina Institute for Reproductive Health (NLIRH)

50 Broad Street, Suite 1937, New York, NY   10004
(212) 422-2553 • fax: (212) 422-2556
e-mail: nlirh@latinainstitute.org
website: http://latinainstitute.org

The National Latina Institute for Reproductive Health (NLIRH) works for reproductive justice for Latinas by addressing common social problems including poverty, unemployment, workplace discrimination, illegal citizenship status, and lack of educational opportunities in the Hispanic American population. The organization achieves its goals by advocating for public policies that benefit Latinas and against those that target low-income women.

National Organization for Women (NOW)

1100 H Street NW, 3rd Floor, Washington, DC   20005
(202) 628-8669 • fax: (202) 785-8576
website: www.now.org

The National Organization for Women (NOW) was founded in 1966. It is the largest and one of the best-known feminist groups in the United States. NOW activism includes electoral lobbying and candidate endorsement, as well as its work in forming policy and bringing legal action on behalf of feminist issues. NOW members also engage in acts of nonviolent civil disobedience such as marches and protests.

National Partnership for Women and Families

1875 Connecticut Avenue NW, Suite 650
Washington, DC   20009
(202) 986-2600 • fax: (202) 986-2539
e-mail: info@nationalpartnership.org
website: www.nationalpartnership.org

The National Partnership for Women and Families was founded in 1971 as the Women's Legal Defense Fund, with the goal of battling sex-based discrimination of all forms in court. In 1998 the group changed its name to reflect its work on behalf of working families, including its long-running push for passage of the Family and Medical Leave Act, which was written by a staff attorney for the group in 1985 and signed into law by former president Bill Clinton in 1993.

National Women's Law Center (NWLC)

11 Dupont Circle NW, #800, Washington, DC   20036
(202) 588-5180 • fax: (202) 588-5185
e-mail: info@nwlc.org
website: www.nwlc.org

The National Women's Law Center (NWLC) was founded in 1972 as part of the Center for Law and Social Policy to address women's issues exclusively. In 1981 it became an independent organization. Among the issues NWLC supports are equal pay and employment, Title IX and education funding, child care and early childhood learning, reproductive rights and access to health care, and women's poverty.

Planned Parenthood Federation of America

434 West Thirty-Third Street, New York, NY   10001
(212) 541-7800 • fax: (212) 245-1845
website: www.plannedparenthood.org

Planned Parenthood was formed as the American Birth Control League in 1921 to promote the use and legalization of birth control in the United States. Currently, Planned Parenthood operates eight hundred clinics across the United States and provides a wide variety of health services to women free of charge.

Women's Campaign Fund (WCF)
1900 L Street NW, Suite 500, Washington, DC   20036
(202) 393-8164 • fax: (202) 393-0649
e-mail: info@wcfonline.org
website: www.wcfonline.org

Women's Campaign Fund (WCF) is dedicated to increasing women's participation in the political process as both voters and candidates. WCF formally endorses candidates and supports them financially through its political action committee. In partnership with its sister organization, the WCF Foundation, the WCF publishes original research reports on the state of women in politics.

Bibliography of Books

Jennifer Baumgardner and Amy Richards — *Manifesta: Young Women, Feminism, and the Future.* New York: Farrar, Straus and Giroux, 2010.

Susan Campbell — *Dating Jesus: A Story of Fundamentalism, Feminism, and the American Girl.* Boston: Beacon Press, 2009.

Gail Collins — *America's Women: Four Hundred Years of Dolls, Drudges, Helpmates, and Heroines.* New York: William Morrow, 2003.

Gail Collins — *When Everything Changed: The Amazing Journey of American Women from 1960 to the Present.* New York: Little, Brown & Co., 2009.

Stephanie Coontz — *A Strange Stirring: The Feminine Mystique and American Women at the Dawn of the 1960s.* New York: Basic Books, 2011.

Rory Dicker — *A History of U.S. Feminisms.* Berkeley, CA: Seal Press, 2008.

Susan J. Douglas — *Enlightened Sexism: The Seductive Message That Feminism's Work Is Done.* New York: Times Books, 2010.

Jan Feldman — *Citizenship, Faith, and Feminism: Jewish and Muslim Women Reclaim Their Rights.* Waltham, MA: Brandeis University Press, 2011.

Estelle B. Freedman, ed.   *The Essential Feminist Reader.* New York: Modern Library, 2007.

Jaclyn Friedman and Jessica Valenti, eds.   *Yes Means Yes! Visions of Female Sexual Power and a World Without Rape.* Berkeley, CA: Seal Press, 2008.

Ayaan Hirsi Ali   *Infidel.* New York: Free Press, 2008.

Lisa Jervis and Andi Zeisler, eds.   *BITCHfest: Ten Years of Cultural Criticism from the Pages of* Bitch *Magazine.* New York: Farrar, Straus and Giroux, 2006.

Ariel Levy   *Female Chauvinist Pigs: Women and the Rise of Raunch Culture.* New York: Free Press, 2006.

Megan Seely   *Fight Like a Girl: How to Be a Fearless Feminist.* New York: New York University Press, 2007.

Deborah Siegel   *Sisterhood, Interrupted: From Radical Women to Grrls Gone Wild.* New York: Palgrave Macmillan, 2007.

Stephanie Staal   *Reading Women: How the Great Books of Feminism Changed My Life.* New York: PublicAffairs, 2011.

Rebecca Traister   *Big Girls Don't Cry: The Election That Changed Everything for American Women.* New York: Free Press, 2010.

Jessica Valenti   *Full Frontal Feminism: A Young Woman's Guide to Why Feminism Matters.* Emeryville, CA: Seal Press, 2007.

Jessica Valenti   *He's a Stud, She's a Slut, and 49 Other Double Standards Every Woman Should Know*. Berkeley, CA: Seal Press, 2008.

Suzanne Venker and Phyllis Schlafly   *The Flipside of Feminism: What Conservative Women Know—and Men Can't Say*. Washington, DC: WND Books, 2011.

Amina Wadud   *Inside the Gender Jihad: Women's Reform in Islam*. London: Oneworld, 2006.

Andi Zeisler   *Feminism and Pop Culture*. Berkeley, CA: Seal Press, 2008.

Index